Contents

Editor's note 8
  Muse, Confidant and Mediator 8
Acknowledgements 11
Forward 12
  Beyond the Basics to Business 12
Introduction 15
  From Good to Great 15
  Evolution of professional practice 16
  Build on your personal experience 17
Chapter 1 - First, set your intentions 19
  A reflection on conflict and resolution, and how they translate to success 19
    Conflict and resolution 21
    How bad do you want it? 22
    The mirror test 23
  The right intentions 23
  Bootstrapping 24
    Chapter Review 26
Chapter 2 - Why do this? 27
  What *moves* you? 27
    Origin story 28
  What is the purpose of your work? 28
  Begin with self-knowledge 30
  What is your growth plan? 31

Accumulation of knowledge 31
The relationship of certification to practice 34
Chapter review 36
Chapter 3 - Defining success 37
How do *you* define success? 37
Consequences of success 39
Happiness as Success 40
Success in the business of hypnotherapy is multi-faceted 40
First is the financial component. 40
Second is the emotional component. 41
Third is reputation and credibility 41
Back to the Future 42
Plan for transition 43
Decide what you want and claim it 45
Develop a relationship with money 46
Ambivalence = Poverty 46
Chapter Review 47
Chapter 4 - What is in it for your client? 49
What value do you hope to give to your clients? 49
Educate. Educate. Educate. 51
What value can you deliver right now? 54
Continuous learning and improvement 58
Chapter Review 60
Chapter 5 - Who is your client? 61
Who will be attracted to you? 61

Make your client a mirror of you 62

Behavior set 63

Attire 65

Competition 66

How to set yourself apart from others 68

    Recovered academic 69

    Recovery story 70

Make yourself unique 70

Certification as a piece of paper or building a skill 71

    Chapter Review 73

Chapter 6 - Who are your peers? 75

How do you position yourself (in hypnotherapy)? 75

Hypnotist or Hypnotherapist? 80

    Chapter Review 82

Chapter 7 - Fees and practice strategy 83

Pick an approach 83

By the hour versus by the program 84

    The way I split up my 20-hour protocol 85

    So, how much is your time worth? 86

    Can you sell it? 86

How busy do you want to be? 87

Profit and Loss 88

    Variables 88

    Fixed costs 88

Pay yourself 89

- Job vs. Profession 90
- You have to *cost* (verb) everything 91
- Actual accounting: Revenue vs Expenses 93
- Business School Primer 94
- Chapter Review 100

Chapter 8 - How to brand YOU 101
- What makes you stand out? 101
- The meaning of the *Dr. Kweethai* brand 101
- Chief Catalyst for Change 103
- Hypnotherapy in branding 104
- Two more things about branding 107
- Creating a market leader: Pitted prunes in the Malaysian market 108
- Marketing strategy 110
- Proficiency and people 111
- Go for the right client 114
- Make it personal 115
  - Chapter review 115
- Lessons from a Roll of Toilet Paper 117

Chapter 9 - What resources do you need? 123
- Set yourself up for success 123
- Resources come in many forms 124
- Bare minimum, you need a dedicated space 124
  - Furniture 126
- Other less than obvious resources 126

What advice, specifically, do you need? 128
Professional Membership & Conferences 130
    Chapter Review 132
Afterword 133
    God Delivers faster than FedEx 133
About the Author 136

Editor's note
Muse, Confidant and Mediator

As of this writing, the author and I have been wife and husband for 15 years. We have also been colleagues, co-authors and business partners. *iHealth Center for Integrated Wellness* is both home and business for us. Our daily commute is fourteen steps from bedroom to office.

We have a semi-formal meeting every morning for thirty to forty-five minutes. Dr. Kweethai with a hot cup of coffee and I with a steaming mug of tea. Much of that time is spent exploring the human condition, i.e., her clients (when she is busy) or life in general (between the busy spells). It is an important collaboration. I have been through hypnotherapy training and passed certification, but have no real desire to practice. Dr. Kweethai, of course, practices at a high level of intensity and effectiveness. We have an arranged marriage; she stands at the front of the room, I take care of the back; it suits our skills and personalities just fine.

Our morning meetings serve two primary purposes, and a third that benefits this book.

1) Dr. Kweethai is a verbal processer. She thinks out loud. Like a sculptor who needs clay in order to form her art, Dr. Kweethai molds ideas as she expresses them verbally. And like the sculptor, it takes time, effort and practice to achieve a masterwork; starting with something rough and unformed, gradually molding and refining, allowing the essence to emerge.

During the morning meetings she re-visits particular themes over and over. Each theme is a lump of clay on the potter's wheel, taking shape with each turn of the wheel. She may think to herself throughout the rest of the day, but the real work can only occur as she sits at the wheel; repetitiously verbalizing the 'clay' until the form and structure is just right.

2) I serve as muse, confidant and mediator. Verbal processing requires an audience; I am a good listener. It is a given that client confidentiality must be maintained; I also preserve the sanctity of Dr. Kweethai's unfinished works (ideas, concepts). As mediator, I provide impartial feedback as she attempts to resolve conflicted versions of a concept.

I can serve these roles because we share a commitment to lifelong learning and intellectual exploration; but also because, as collaborators, our individual roles are mutually beneficial.

3) Dr. Kweethai wanted this book to be in her voice. It's a noble objective, but as former editor of a professional journal, I pulled rank on this one. It's *mostly* in her voice.

Dr. Kweethai's primary strengths are derived from being a verbal processor and highly relational. Audiences and individual clients love her. It is hard to translate that infectious spirit onto the written page.

It is a delicate balance to translate the spoken word into prose. Good prose makes up for the absence of non-verbal communication we experience with a live speaker. There are words used in writing that rarely come out in conversation. Those words still have to be consistent with the speaker and what she wants to convey.

In this book, I use my experience as muse, confidant and mediator to inform word choices, remaining as close as practicable to Dr. Kweethai's *in vivo* language and meaning.

3a) Content within this book derives from two sources.

1) The basic content is directed at the aspiring entrepreneur who intends to build a successful business practice doing hypnotherapy. The content is not comprehensive, but that is sort of the point; Dr. Kweethai has read hundreds of books in the process of developing her hypnotherapy skills and the business practice. Note "in the process of;" she did not wait until she was all-knowing to begin, she began as soon as she earned certification and learned along the way. We anticipate you will do likewise.

2) Dr. Kweethai is a natural storyteller and raconteur. Stories in this book come, naturally, from her experience. Though many are success stories, some describe hiccups along the way. The point is that we do what we advise students and clients to do; work hard, work smart, do good work, and success naturally follows. That is where the stories come from.

In most cases throughout the book, stories are inset from the main text. I chose this as a literary device to distinguish between "I" and "You." "I" is Dr. Kweethai describing her own experiences. "You" refers to the reader. We realize all readers come to this book with unique backgrounds and experience, so "You" is a very generic pronoun.

I have tried to be gender-sensitive. She and he are used randomly wherever a more vague pronoun (they, them, their) had the potential to be confusing.

Other editors may take exception to my inclusion of contractions, generally a no-no in formal literature. It's fine with me if that's the only editorial bone they pick at. I find it a way to maintain a conversational, accessible tone. I hope you agree.

Steve Stork, EdD, May 2015

Acknowledgements

My first thank you is to my editor, who is also husband, muse, and business partner, Dr. Steve Stork. Without your left hand, my right hand could not have written this book. I am grateful to you, the reader, for this book is written for you. The substance upon which the content of this book is built is the sum total of the generous help and encouragement of those who have trusted and believed in me; mentors, teachers, clients and students. In particular, thank you Linda and Robert Otto for embracing Steve and me into IMDHA. Thank you to senior colleagues in the field who have taught me formally and informally, and also gifted me with your friendship: George Bien, Philip Holder, Roy Hunter, Richard Nongard, Scott Sandland, Michael Watson and many others. Thank you Gil Boyne (deceased), who continues to guide me from the other side. And Jerry Brandt, you do not know how much your kindness meant to me as I began. I am grateful to loyal students, such as Dr. Umesh Tiwari, MD, who continues to study with me long after certification. And, thank you, GOD; the people you send to me make this work possible. I am grateful as I continue the journey.

Kweethai Neill, PhD

May 2015

Forward
Beyond the Basics to Business

In the beginning years of my practice, I knew there was something lacking in my training as a hypnotherapist. At the completion of my basic certification program, I remember the instructor telling us we were on our own and not to call her in the future. I was shocked. I felt alone and naked, having just plunged into a whole new arena of work.

It contradicted what I had experienced as an academic. When I passed my doctoral defense (the final oral examination for a PhD), my professor shook my hand, embraced me, and stated proudly, "Congratulations, Dr. Neill. Welcome to our community of scholars." Wow, what a difference!

As an academic, I was warmly invited to become part of an established community. As a hypnotherapist, I was thrown into the world with no support. With twenty-seven days of training I was expected to make a living helping other people. Yikes!

I knew in my gut there was something fierce missing in that equation, but I could not articulate it at the time. Perhaps my instructor wanted to launch me like a mother bird who kicks her young off the nest. I could fall to the ground and die, or I could flap my wings and take flight. Eleven years of successful practice later I can say I took flight, although it was not entirely easy. I might say that my success *was in spite of* rather than *because of* the way I was launched.

Over the years I have been blessed by the generosity of newfound friends, mentors and colleagues who helped me when I screamed for assistance. There are too many to name but a few stand out. Gil Boyne was my primary mentor. I learned much from him about hypnotherapy, but also benefitted from his wisdom related to handling challenges in my life. Another early savior, friend and colleague was Jerry Brandt. He was my first partner in a clinical practicum as part of a Master Class with Gil. Jerry gave me many great suggestions when I asked for help in cases that puzzled me.

As a lifelong learner I have partaken in numerous trainings; some with illustrious teachers; some with instructors who were not so illustrious. I learned what to do from the former and what **not** to do from the latter.

Whereas basic certification training serves as a good start, there is much, much more to learn in order to be an effective and successful hypnotherapist. Mastery of the skills to do good work is critical, but to make a successful living from hypnotherapy requires business acumen. During the time I provided training in my own hypnotherapy school, a prominent feature of my curriculum was coursework in business. That is something I have found lacking in training programs that focus on getting students certified in the shortest possible time.

After eleven years of full time practice, I feel I have acquired some useful information to share with hypnotherapy colleagues who wish to build and sustain a successful practice. Success has a different meaning to everyone. I share my idea of success here with you. In broad terms, a successful practice has to be financially viable (bringing in enough revenue to pay expenses and yourself, with some to spare) and spiritually meaningful (actually helping the clients you serve).

In the pages that follow I share my insights, experience and knowledge with you. I include some simple exercises as a call to action to get you on the way to a successful practice.

I am not proposing my way as the only road to success. I know of hypnotherapy colleagues who make more money than I do, and sell more products. Others see more clients and teach more students. It is not a contest. I am submitting one point of view...mine. It comes from eleven years of joyful, meaningful and financially positive hypnotherapy practice. It has been an amazing journey and I look forward to many more years of serving clients with my best work, adding value and joy to their lives.

Hypnotherapy is a unique enough field that perhaps it will always require a leap of faith. As you get pushed from the safety of the nest, there will of necessity always be some furious wing-flapping. My intention for this book is to help you catch the wind quickly so you can fly confidently toward the sky.

Thank you for trusting me as your guide in this journey. Let's begin.

Kweethai Neill, PhD., May 2015

Introduction
From Good to Great

In any level of business, you have to start somewhere. Maybe you just completed your training, passed the certification exam and are ready to see clients. Maybe you have an existing practice you would like to see do better. This book is not just for beginners. It is for anyone who wants to practice **differently;** whether newly certified or promoting yourself from hobbyist to fulltime professional.

Wherever you are in your practice, I advise you to use this book as a new start. Unless you already earn 6 figures and are reading this book as a distraction, if you want to effectively engage new habits to get there, you are going to have to start at the beginning.

If you have an established practice that is going "well enough," use this book to take it from good to great. If you are just getting started, this book will help you learn from my mistakes, not yours. Somewhere in the middle (just plain stuck) and looking for a new direction? This book is for you!

Likewise, you can start at whatever level of skill you have acquired. You need to have completed your initial hypnotherapy training to understand some of the recommendations in this book (since it is specific to the business of hypnotherapy). Beyond that, I understand that hypnotherapists come in many stripes.

> Throughout this book I give examples from my own practice. That practice is based on my *iChange Therapy* process and a 20-hour protocol. I do not expect you to practice that way. It works for me. That is what is important. My methodology evolved over a decade and my practice evolved with it. I have continuously reflected on

the nature of my skills, the way I practice, the ways I convey that to clients, and a fee base consistent with the level of value and service I provide.

Evolution of professional practice

Hypnotherapy training programs typically address specific symptoms, affecting certain outcomes. A client who smokes wants to become a non-smoker. A client with a phobia of snakes wants to be able to walk through the jungle and not jump ten feet every time something that resembles a snake appears in his path. Those are clear and specific challenges that clients present. Most schools teach how to address those issues in a traditional hypnotherapy practice.

> What has evolved in my hypnotherapy practice; largely because I am a health educator, scientist and researcher, but also through observation and self-reflection based on working with clients; I realize that managing a symptom may be well and good, but it doesn't really address the core issue that underscores the client's maladaptive behavior.

Symptom management is like the carnival game Whack-a-Mole. As you take care of one symptom another appears, but in a different form. A client says she wants to quit smoking and becomes a non-smoker after a session or two, so technically she is done. But the issues that underscore her smoking behavior—which generally is a negative way of coping with stress—are not addressed. It is highly likely new maladaptive behaviors will emerge.

> I prefer to do deeper work, to go after the emotional issues underlying the symptoms. I address the source of fears that are causing the negative coping skills. Over the years clients have asked me to address this and that, but then get engaged in the full process under my guidance. We rarely

even talk about the original issues. At the very end the client is surprised to realize those behaviors have disappeared without having been directly addressed. Once the fears are resolved, the rest takes care of itself.

Build on your personal experience

It is very helpful, though not a requirement, but strongly advised, that you believe in and trust the work. Whether or not you have to experience it from a client perspective is debatable; however, it is very helpful for the therapist to know what it feels like to be in the other chair. That's not to say that every surgeon should have gone through surgery prior to cutting into a patient. However, surgeons with some first-hand experience are better able to appreciate the anxiety patients experience. And while I agree every experience in hypnosis is unique; you can't describe it at all—or at least honestly—without some degree of first-hand experience.

Since hypnosis is so highly experiential, personal and private, it requires a very high degree of trust. What better way to convince a client than to have walked the walk yourself. "I don't know exactly how you feel, but I have an idea for what it feels like when you feel something lacking in your life, as you describe it. I have been there and I know this process has helped me. So there is a good chance it can help you."

Chapter 1 - First, set your intentions
A reflection on conflict and resolution, and how they translate to success

While writing this book I reflected a lot on what success means to me. Of course, you have to arrive at your own definition and rationale, but what follows are some thoughts that occurred to me. It is part of my personal script. Not that I recite it in its entirety to every client; but each client may hear bits of it that are appropriate to their particular needs or situation. To be clear, I don't *recite* these things at all, it's just that, since they come up so regularly, it comes out pretty similar each time I go to it.

I recommend that you develop your own origin story. The purpose is not to bore clients with your own issues or pat yourself on the back. Rather, the client should hear that in conflict there is always an opportunity for resolution.

The conflict you, dear reader, face right now is the challenge of migrating into fulltime, highly successful practice. I have been there. Here is my story of resolution.

As I closed the door behind me on academia, I breathed a breath of fresh air, a sensation of freedom. I saw no boundaries to the expression of my work and creative energies. I had no idea where that would lead, but I felt a sense of oneness, peace with the universe, trusting that something would evolve to give me a sense of freedom when I work.

As I encountered hypnotherapy, it became more possible for me to describe, with some specificity, what my life sometime in the future would look like; that is, having what I wanted. "A client arrives at my office having engaged a contract to participate in a therapy process of my own design. The client trusts me entirely to lead her out of her pit of darkness, executing the contract. I have total freedom to manage my time with the client and 'deal with what emerges' with unbounded creativity. I go no-holds-barred in the therapy room with the client. I pull out whatever I know, and then some, to help her. My process is creative and liberating. The results are astounding. As positive change occurs in the client, I experience a deep sense of satisfaction and peace; worthiness I cannot describe. It is a phenomenal feeling that my life has meaning."

When I first conceived that description, iCHANGE THERAPY was still emerging as my methodology and I still did mostly two-hour sessions. I did not know *exactly* how some aspects of the description would emerge, yet I stated it in present tense, knowing that the description itself was what I wanted. I then opened myself to whatever form its realization might take. In other words, I opened myself to change.

You might ask how I recognize the right changes as they occur. Time and again throughout my life I have been challenged with difficult choices, and I tend to take the road less traveled. I acknowledge that such an approach tends to a put lot at stake and create the appearance of unnecessary difficulty; but when I walk through that wall of fear I always find a feeling of peace and calm on the other side. Midway through the wall is a state of conflict that is exhilarating; quiet and noisy at the same time. As I inevitably emerge into a state of resolution I experience a clear tone, a brilliant color energy.

The sequence of conflict leading to resolution has happened often enough in my life that I now easily identify it. I felt it as I conceived both my daughters. I felt it with Steve, as our relationship migrated from friendship into marriage. I knew he was the individual I would spend the rest of my life with. I walked away from an internship at the Cleveland Clinic, despite an earlier struggle to get in. Throughout each crucial turn in my life, the tension of conflict has been followed by the peace of resolution, like the calm after a storm. Each emergence testifies to a better of two options.

There is a backstory to each of those circumstances; suffice for now that at each occurrence I would say to myself that I should be so scared. But I was not scared. And that made me scared that I was not scared when I thought I should be scared but was not. In that moment of perfect clarity I know I have done the right thing.

Recently I disengaged from a friendship that I had thought was a good one. I felt bad about detaching from a friend, but then realized it was not in the best interest of my soul to try and make a silk purse out of a sow's ear. It was scary because it meant ditching some business interactions and networking opportunities, but I walked away with a sense of calm. He was, after all not really a friend, and so I was not abandoning a friend, only leaving a lie.

Conflict and resolution
Within conflict is the necessity of getting over limiting beliefs. There has to be a certain tension in that crux. Do I do it? Do I not do it?

It's like getting up in the morning to exercise. Do I want to do it? Do I not want to do it? Instead of wasting time perseverating on the debate inside my head, I just get up and do it. As I sweat and feel good, by the time I am done, I am grateful to have done it.

To recap, when you make a tough choice, there is tension, conflict, fear and anxiety. When I know deep in my gut what I need to do, that is what I must do. As I push myself through it the fear dissipates and is over. Peace ensues.

How bad do you want it?
I remember the first time I jumped off a three-meter diving board into a twenty-foot deep diving pool. I climbed all the way to the top platform and walked tentatively to the very edge of the diving board. Preparing to jump, I turned backwards and balanced on my toes. It was very scary; but I knew if I did not jump pretty soon I would not be given the opportunity to do it again. Despite a momentary conflict, there really was no other decision; I was committed to jump, no matter if I drowned. So I pushed off the board and immediately descended into the pool. It was a small slice of time, traveling ten feet before meeting the water, but it seemed like forever.

If you are going to make a business you really have to jump off the diving board. You have to make a commitment. It is better to do it now than to stand on the edge of the board and wonder. Or worse, some never even get to the edge. They wonder at the audacity of those who do; or they remain aloof from it with the rationalization, "I could do that too, if I really wanted to." But they avoid putting themselves in close enough proximity to ever be faced with the chance to choose.

To be successful you cannot go about something halfhearted. I did a luncheon presentation called "Hobby or Business." Of the forty or so hypnotherapists attending, only two hands raised when I asked who was in full-time practice. And only one of those two was making a living at it.

What is wrong with that picture? After all, it is a skewed sample; a professional conference. Do only people who dabble in hypnotherapy attend conferences? Maybe others are too busy practicing.

Would you, as a client, pay a professional fee to a weekend practitioner, someone who only dabbles in the art? Put in another context, would you see a doctor who practices medicine as a hobby? For a comparable fee, you are much more likely go next door to the MD with a waiting room full of patients.

The mirror test

Stand in front of a mirror and look at yourself. Would you consult a hypnotherapist who looks like you, talks like you, or practices like you?

If you want to be a successful entrepreneur, you have to first be willing to invest in yourself. You have to be your biggest investment. You have to be your first best customer. You have to turn your eyeballs the other way around and look inside to see if you would engage a person like yourself, and pay the fees you ask your clients to pay. Would you do what you ask your clients to do?

The right intentions

Do not be too concerned if you do not get it exactly right on the first go. It is akin to dating. It is more important to set the intention right. Let me share how applying the right intentions found me a great companion.

> Recently divorced and newly single, I found myself dating. Friends dragged me to singles parties. I didn't know such things existed, I had been married so long. I no longer knew how to date, let alone how to handle a singles party. I worried about predators, or that the next person I talked to might expect me to engage in activities I was not ready for. I found it all rather strange.

> After being asked out a few times and dating a bit, I got tired of kissing frogs. I did not like the dating scene, trolling for a date. Some girlfriends liked to go to a bar. Why would I want to do that? I didn't like to drink and I had just left a

spouse who drank too much; why would I sit at a bar with the hope that someone would buy me a drink? I could buy my own drinks if I wanted to drink. And even if someone bought a drink for me, I would not enjoy it. To me that whole concept is insanity.

One day I came to the conclusion that I just wanted one good partner. I wanted a companion. It didn't matter if it was a dog or a woman or a man. I preferred a man, one man; that we could end up as life partners totally committed in marriage.

So I sat down and applied my own marketing principles. What were the features and benefits I wanted from a partner? "God, as long as you are looking, here's my shopping list." I filled a page and looked at it. It occurred to me that the things I was looking for in a companion I had to be able to offer. I had to first know me. (Back to marketing principles, you first have to know your product; what proficiency and skills you have to offer.) When I realized I could check off every item I desired, and be able to offer it first, my spouse happened.

At this writing I have been happily married 15 years. We have been very happy because I knew what I wanted and I knew what I had to offer. We are best of friends.

Bootstrapping

In 1990 I was recently divorced, and broke. I moved from northeast Ohio to take a position in Texas at Sam Houston State University for $30,000 a year. I asked the Dean to give me one additional dollar from his own pocket. It was to signify that 1) he would have paid me more if he could and 2) I would work hard for every dollar I received. Twenty years later, having worked for two other universities, and now with a fulltime practice in clinical hypnotherapy; my financial planner tells me that I can work by choice, meaning I am out of the rat race! He told me I could retire today if I wanted to.

I did not earn it all in hypnotherapy, but good habits I had been growing since childhood kicked in so that every new dollar has been put to its best advantage. Some business books claim you need to spend money in order to make money. My experience is that you need to spend the money that needs to be spent and save the money that needs to be saved. And, invest in things you know. The talent is to be discerning so you make the right choices.

I have paid for training trips. I have paid for expensive consultations. I have invested in website development. I have also put money into dud advertising. I have taken risks and learned from them. Some ventures pan out and others do not. It is called the *practical school of business!*

I have been my own banker in anything I've ever done. I taught cooking classes to pay for my thesis research. I saved up my own money to launch my business projects and financed my own endeavors.

It is a great feeling not to owe money to the bank or be financially obligated to family and friends. Owing money to others devalues the relationship. Financial freedom translates to spiritual freedom. It is great to be debt free.

However, sometimes it is not practical to be your own banker. A long time ago a banker friend gave me some very sound advice. She was a second generation banker in a very small town in rural Ohio. She told me that if I ever had to borrow money, there were only three legitimate reasons. 1) To put a roof over your head (as in a house mortgage). 2) To acquire tools to make a living (those tools include knowledge [education and training] as well as physical equipment). 3) For transportation to get to work (car loan, train or bus fares, pay a neighbor).

Notice, luxuries don't count. "Borrow only for what you need, work for what you want." If and when you start to get ahead, put that bit of largesse into a contingency fund for medical emergencies. Then, if you do not plan to work forever, it is prudent to save for retirement. That is a whole other story. Let's get to a 6 figure practice first.

Chapter Review

Some wise person once said, when you first don't get it right, try and try again. I don't believe in trying.

I believe that when first you don't get it right, STOP, take time to assess the process and then do it again with a better idea. If you do the same thing over and over again and expect the different results, it is called insanity. This goes for business as well as life.

Chapter 2 - Why do this?

What *moves* you?

There is a big difference between being an artist; having a high level of art or skill; and being able to make a living out of it. Making a living has to do with running a business; entrepreneurship. That is something most people have not considered.

To become a hypnotherapist there has to be some driving force. As Gil Boyne used to say, "You need that fire in your belly." Maybe you once had personal issues that you overcame with the help of a hypnotherapist and you got inspired by the work. Or, you saw how effective it was for people you know, and you thought you could do it as well.

What else do you know about yourself? How well do you know yourself? Only the answers to such questions can reliably explain why you are doing this. Only some hypnotherapists get rich, so it can't be an income motive. A service orientation makes more sense. Or, it can be both a service and a way to make money, but you have to figure out how to integrate them.

For most the practice of hypnotherapy is a second career. People don't just jump out of high school into hypnotherapy; though I know a few who have and have been successful. It is more common that you have already done something else in your life.

If you had a successful career prior to hypnotherapy, what moved you to leave something that had worked for you (even if it just produced an income) to do something new? What drove you to become a hypnotherapist? Make sure that is in your origin story.

Origin story

> To develop trust, potential clients need to know a little about you. In fact, they will very often ask, "How did you get into that?" Use that opportunity to tell your 'origin story'. "Yes, I was in another field. Then I discovered hypnotherapy and found it appealing. So I completed the training, became certified, and now I specialize in ... because ..." Plan it, but try not to sound rehearsed. The goal is to promote trust in both you and the work.

Successful entrepreneurs are powerfully drawn to do what they do. It is not easy to be an entrepreneur. If you think you are just going to leave your job, open a business, and make lots of money with very little work, you are totally living in Egypt. It is the reverse.

To be an entrepreneur means long hours, sometimes not getting paid. It may take months before you see any financial results. You will pour a lot of money in before the first dollar comes out. Unless you have something more compelling than a paycheck to motivate you, you may as well keep your job. You have to identify that driving force. What moves you to want to do this above everything else?

Whatever the reason, your 'origin' story helps you stay focused on the work. It also helps you market your work. There is nothing more compelling than an original success story.

What is the purpose of your work?

It is critical to find your big purpose. Despite the title of this book, money cannot serve as your main purpose. Yes, there has to be financial viability for your business to be sustainable; but if all you want is to make a living and pay bills, there are easier ways to cover your living expenses.

Any business that expends more money than it brings in is not a sustainable business, it is a hobby. Even if you allocate money from other sources to subsidize your practice (*a la* financial CPR), the practice itself is not financially viable. When a human being ceases to breathe the rest is moot. A business that cannot turn a profit—revenues do not exceed expenses—is in code blue. No breathing = no life. No profits = No business.

> That sounds very severe, but it is amazing to me how many hypnotherapists approach the business of a hypnotherapy practice with the calm assurance that it will fail. As I describe to them the things that have worked for me over the years, they reply with excuses about how it cannot work for them. In effect, they are in a state of paralysis, unable to launch the business fulltime because they are so sure it will not produce enough income to be worthwhile; and therefore practicing very little and accepting a pittance when they do.

Yes, any business has to be financially sustainable, but what will sustain **you**? What do **you** want from the practice of hypnotherapy?

What are the personal benefits you hope to derive from your business? What kind of intellectual and creative benefits might you desire? If you practice as most training programs advocate—following a set protocol and accepting a 'minimum wage' as it were—how is that different from a job?

The way to a 6-figure practice is to recognize the art in applying the science of hypnotherapy. Artists apply themselves for the sheer enjoyment of practicing their art. Yes, it takes a bit of savvy to get rich while plying one's art, but if you don't you still have the satisfaction of remaining true to that art. That makes life worthwhile.

So, in what ways can you anticipate the opportunity to stand back, admire your work, smile and congratulate yourself on a good job? As a hypnotherapist you must be able to derive a sense of satisfaction from being able to help clients and give them value. How you measure that is highly subjective; but you have to know that your work works.

> While working with a client I know at the end of the day I get to see the results. The client always gains something as a result of her interaction with me. And the benefits exceed the amount of money she paid me. I also help the client value the changes she has accomplished.

Begin with self-knowledge

Confidence begins with self-knowledge. The foundation of leadership is self-mastery. As the therapist, you have to first be your own best customer.

The following are questions you need to ask yourself to determine if you are ready to 1) practice, 2) do hypnotherapy fulltime, and 3) open a business and be successfully self-employed.

- Are you ready to see clients?
- Are you ready for fulltime practice?
- Can you make it as an entrepreneur?
- What is your current practice capability?

As hypnotherapy is not a licensed profession, it should come as no surprise that organizations and schools certify at different levels, that some emphasize different skills and modes of practice, and that clinical experience varies widely. Whatever the nature of your training, ultimately the quality of practice depends on the quality of your skills and your level of confidence in them.

Hypnotherapists experience their own placebo effect. If you believe your work to be effective, it will be effective. If you don't, it won't.

What is your growth plan?
Wherever and whatever you learned that led to certification, do not stop learning. Keep learning from many teachers.

Keep always in mind *why* what you are engaged in is called a practice. Every client presents a unique experience to learn from. All you can do is your very best. But over time, your best should progressively get better.

Whenever you find yourself unsure of what you are doing, take that as a sign you need more training, then go get it.

Accumulation of knowledge
There is a difference between the teacher who teaches twenty years and the teacher who teaches one year twenty times. If you practice the way you were taught, and that is all you ever do, and you don't reflect in a way that leads to better practice; or even worse, you work from scripts that you never stray from or modify; after fifteen to twenty years of practice your skills will not have improved. There are no seniority increases in private practice; that means there is no rationale to increase fees commensurate with your 'experience' if your abilities have not changed.

It's a matter of personal goals. I have met hypnotherapists who specialize in a few issues. They record a script and put headphones on the client. They have multiple rooms, each with a comfortable chair. The hypnotherapist spends only a few minutes before and after the recording with the client. Although it works for a lot of clients, the hypnotherapist is only minimally engaged. Without seeing the client, the therapist is unaware of other signs in the client's behavior or demeanor that would give clues to underlying issues. Maybe that is not important when the emphasis is on efficiently processing a high volume of clients or delivering a canned program.

If that is the style of practice you want, it can work (and obviously does work for many hypnotherapists); and it can make a lot of money. But it has a tendency to grind you down. You cannot charge as high an hourly rate because it is superficial work. And you need a constant influx of new clients. With that many clients, you are probably going to need a larger space, more equipment, a receptionist, etc. That effects the balance between how much money you bring in versus how much you get to keep.

You also have to consult your moral compass. In what way do you define success for yourself? It is highly subjective. Money is just one of many variables.

You can make a six-figure income by opening more offices and working sixty hours a week year after year with an arbitrary goal of continuing to increase the number of clients you see. Or…you can have a six-figure income seeing one client a month. It is not just a matter of personal choice. It is how you want to apply yourself. Knowledge is power. By increasing your knowledge and skill you can increase your fees, either to earn more working the same number of hours, or to make the same amount of money working fewer hours. You make the choice.

> I do not want to see clients back-to-back every day. I would rather my work have meaning. IChange Therapy has been my way of carving out what is meaningful for me. The **meaningfulness** of business is something that few people discuss or consider when they are starting a business. I flush

that out when doing a live workshop because everyone is different. It's a piece I was never taught. Rather, it just evolved as a consequence of my self- and continuous-improvement ethic.

Schools have a limited scope in delivering a curriculum. At the end of instruction students are assessed to verify that they have learned what is in the curriculum. The end is called Commencement. But the true entrepreneurial spirit is expressed when you take Commencement not as an ending but as a platform for launch. That is where you set goals, consider possibilities, and set an alternative and new course.

Going back in history, it has been called apprenticeship. The apprentice learns the techniques of an art form, doing practical work for a period usually measured in years under the supervision of a master. The creation of that art on one's own occupies a rather long period between apprenticeship and becoming a master oneself. If you are very diligent, with a little luck, you may develop your own style of the art in the process.

> I have discovered, as an academic, something lacking in many academic programs. Students comply with hours and days of training, only to receive a piece of paper that documents little more than that they sat through the required hours. Many people think that the piece of paper, or being certified by a particular organization, gives you the license to practice. Well...it does...but it is just a piece of paper.

> A month before I received my doctorate in philosophy I asked my residency professor what it meant to have a doctorate in philosophy. Up to that point I had never taken a course in philosophy. I was to have PhD after my name, designating a doctorate in philosophy, but I had never studied philosophy. Now, in graduate school if you ask a

question and the professor does not have the answer, it's common to hear, "Well, Kweethai, it will be your job to discuss that question next seminar." So I was left to ponder what it meant.

What meaning is there in the piece of paper that tells the world you are certified in clinical hypnotherapy? What does it mean to the client who sees it framed and hanging on your office wall? What kind of expectation can she have?

Self-knowledge, self-awareness and self-reflection; when formal education ends, these are the traits that support and guide the unending journey of continuous improvement.

The relationship of certification to practice

The meaning you attach to certification determines what you feel comfortable charging and how you position yourself. As highly qualified as you may have been in a prior field, the certification process does not include mentorship as part of the induction into hypnotherapy; you have to create that opportunity yourself. Finding your own mentor is part of the process of becoming comfortable practicing.

> Two weeks before taking the ACHE (American Council of Hypnotist Examiners) certification exam, I bought an office property. The ink on my certificate was still drying when I opened my door as *iHealth Center for Integrated Wellness*. I was Dr. Kweethai Neill, certified clinical hypnotherapist.
>
> It took years of hard study to earn a PhD. I was to learn that the process redefined me as a professor. In contrast, hypnotherapy training consumed a few hundred hours of formal training. As the certificate stated 500 hours, I presume the instructor included all the books on the reading list; which I dutifully read, but knew many classmates did not since there was no accountability related

to that so-called *requirement*. (Their problem, not mine.) Five hundred hours seems like a big number, but I was initially unsure what I was supposed be able to do. I can only imagine the confusion of classmates who completed only the bare requirements. Add to that, as we finished, the instructor told us we were on my own, and not to call her.

Hypnotherapy was a new world where I didn't know anyone. I had attended conferences and mingled with peers during my academic career. That now made me feel even more isolated since I no longer had access to a familiar community with whom to consult. I was on my own trying to figure it out, but I had two advantages. 1) I had already been thru the process when I transformed from stay-at-home mom and graduate student to Professor. 2) Having completed all the requirements of the training course, and then some, I was confident in my ability to practice.

I was accustomed to teaching. Looking into the future, I knew that if and when I started a hypnotherapy school, it would include a mentoring component to continue after certification was complete. It would create a sense of continuity beyond certification, to help new hypnotherapists transition into practice.

For the time being, I created my own community to consult. Gil Boyne and Jerry Brandt were to prove supportive and generous when I called upon them for help. If I have any talent at all, it has been a lifelong ability to recognize talent and tap into it.

I subsequently developed relationships with other mentors; facilitating my transformation from professor to hypnotherapist, and eventually to *Chief Catalyst for Change*.

Chapter review

Many new hypnotherapists struggle with the notion of success because they do not know themselves and have no relevant purpose. They have attached some romantic notion to hypnotherapy, without fully comprehending the level of skill and knowledge, much less personal confidence, it takes to practice successfully.

This chapter has presented some open-ended questions for you to consider. In the following chapters you will complete a few simple exercises to answer those questions in ways that are concrete enough to build your business upon a solid foundation.

Chapter 3 - Defining success

"Good enough never is." Mrs. Fields

How do *you* define success?
In the process of earning certification, did you ever pause to consider how you might define a successful hypnotherapy practice, or did you just flow from the training into the work. Once you find yourself in the thick of practice, it is less easy to step back and consider, with a sense of clarity, what you want out of it.

When launching a business, it is a positive sign if it feels like a good fit; but that could be misleading. Frequent references within this book remind you to differentiate business from hobby.

> By all outward indications Annette had a solid business. She had an attractive office, was known throughout the community, and serviced a steady flow of clients. Her CPA told another story, "Annette, you don't have a business; you are operating a hobby." She provided unlimited access to her time for a small upfront fee. Of course clients loved her; it amounted to free counseling. Free? It turns out she billed clients who subsequently failed to pay. She considered 'accounts receivable' as income; her CPA counted them as what they really were, 'services rendered without payment'. Thus, a hobby where you pay to practice… like golf.

From a practical perspective, to work toward success you have to sit down and flush out—with a sense of specificity and clarity—what success really means to you, what you want out of your practice as a business enterprise.

I ask *business advisory* clients how much money they need to earn in order to feel successful. Some pluck a number out of the air, like "a million dollars." So I probe further, "...and if a million dollars floated out of the sky and landed on you today, what would you need it for?" Most haven't a clue. That makes it the wrong answer.

I specifically use the word 'feel' instead of 'think'. How do you 'feel' successful? We are conditioned by the prevailing culture to 'think' a million dollars equates to success. But if you think about it, "a million dollars" so far exceeds the needs of a normal person that you could easily be successful and happy on much less. So few people can accurately perceive "a million dollars" that it has no logical value.

Money is nothing more than a medium of exchange. A million dollars in your bank account does not make you a million times happier than when you didn't have a million dollars. Yet, while money is only one possible measure of success, most people consider it a singular message.

Yes, we imagine what a million dollars could buy and that those things might make us a little happier. But really, they are just things; and when you start striving for things to make you happy instead of examining what it really means to be happy, you step on the treadmill of one-upmanship. Just as you acquire the object of your desire a new bauble catches your eye. You convince yourself you cannot be happy until you have acquired it. And when you have, there is yet another bauble. When one-upping yourself there is no endpoint.

John Bogle, in his book ***Enough: True Measures of Money, Business, and Life***, explains that happiness can only be achieved when you come to the realization that you have enough. Enough of what? It does not matter. When you no longer need or want, you have enough.

I know people with larger homes and fancier cars than mine who eat at expensive restaurants and go on extravagant vacations. I do not envy them. Neither do I criticize them. I could upgrade my lifestyle if I chose to; but that is not my measure of success.

I have enough. I am happy. I have made enough money to 'feel' successful. How close I am to "a million dollars" is irrelevant.

So, how will you *feel* when you have achieved success? When you can define it, you then work backwards and strategize how to get there.

Consequences of success

In some ways making a lot of money creates as many problems as it solves. Imagine having to protect a million dollars. Many lottery winners spend the money quickly and research indicates they end up worse off in terms of how they feel about themselves than before they hit the jackpot.

A mansion requires a security system to keep riff-raff from breaking in. The rich are also constantly worried about Uncle Sam's share. I knew a guy who was making enough money that his tax bill exceeded $150,000. Instead of enjoying his good fortune with what remained, he spent his free time researching risky tax shelters and investing in them. In the end, it was a market he did not understand and he lost his shirt. Today, in a negative financial position, he no longer worries about speculative investments and questionable tax write-offs. Rather, he struggles to pay his bills at the end of the month.

So what's it going to be? Worry about paying a lot of taxes in order to protect your money? Or, worry over having no money, and hope for a big tax refund each spring. Of course, living without worry is the preferable third choice.

Clearly money is not everything. If you don't know what happiness is, it doesn't matter if your bank account is either empty or bursting.

Happiness as Success
At the end of the day, the definition of success is an emotional state. In hypnotherapy the outcome is a qualitative difference in how clients feel as each session ends. For the hypnotherapist, then, any time you help a client feel better leaving your office than when they came in, that is success. To what degree a client feels better is debatable. That is something to negotiate with the client early in the session, so you both know what you want out of it.

Success in the business of hypnotherapy is multi-faceted
First is the financial component.
Finances are critical when running a business. Financial viability means more money is coming in than going out. If you don't understand that simple equation, take a basic accounting class.

Even if you keep an accountant on retainer, as the business owner you have to be able to read a balance sheet, create a monthly profit and loss statement, and know how much money you have in the bank. Otherwise, how can you set relevant and appropriate goals for your business? For example, how many clients do you need to see each month, and at what fee, to cover your bills and give yourself a salary? If you are reading this book, you aspire to 6 figures, not minimum wage. If you do not pay yourself as much as a Walmart employee, you should shut down your business and get a job at Walmart.

Many part-time hypnotherapists use money from other resources to support their hypnotherapy practice. Maybe it is from another job or from a spouse in a higher-income position. Either way, that is not the way to run a business, it simply supports hypnotherapy as a hobby.

Yes, I have stated earlier that money is a poor measure of success. But that is only when you place too much emphasis on it. At the other extreme is allowing a dearth of money to support you in poverty. This book helps you to aspire to a 6-figure income. If you want to donate your time and service, and live like a monk, find another book (and, no, I will not be writing it!)

Second is the emotional component.
Does 1) hypnotherapy and 2) your hypnotherapy practice (the business) make your heart sing? Doing what you do, in the time you do it; does it make your soul smile? Knowing that your work has helped someone in a way far more valuable than the money they paid you is priceless. Well...the price is that you also have to take pride in a thriving business, otherwise you won't be in a position to help anyone.

Third is reputation and credibility
How do you feel about yourself when you walk out of your house into the community? Do you have a sense of pride and satisfaction in being who you are, doing what you do?

There are probably more, but those are the main pillars of success.

Back to the Future

So, how much money do you want to make? How much do you think your work is worth? Set a price.

Explore the basic nuts and bolts of a basic business operation. Then collect numbers on how much each nut and bolt costs in your location, and how much you can sell it for.

- Estimate start-up costs for equipment and furniture, as well as soap and paint.
- Research real estate (whether you plan to rent or buy, it's always Location, Location, Location) and local utility costs.
- Strategic planning begins with studying the demographics of your surrounding community. Average income and housing costs are a good place to start.
- Then analyze the local market potential for your service. Do some 'long-tail' internet searches—i.e., "service" + "location"—to find out how many local people are looking for your service.
- Check out the competition to get an idea of practice methods and prevailing rates.

Put numbers to all of it and start to build a budget.

- How much money do you need to make in order to pay your basic business expenses?
- How much, in salary, do you need to make each month to live on?
- How many clients do you need, each week, month or year; and at what rate of payment; to bring in sufficient income?
- What other products can you offer to supplement that income?

In my first year of practice I replaced my university income. That was necessary because I had given up a good job. At the time I could easily have gone back to a new position at another university, but the hypnotherapy practice gave me something that working in a university did not.

Plan for transition

Someone questioned me about giving up my career and stepping off the mountain. At the time I did not have the luxury of choice. I didn't know I was going to become a hypnotherapist. I was responding to a call of my soul. What I was doing as an administrator did not serve my soul's purpose. I didn't know what the alternative would be, but I had to shut one down before the other could appear.

I did not have the luxury of aiming for a soft landing as I leapt out of higher education. Looking backward, after earning hypnotherapy certification and a year of practice, I could have still gone back and opted for a position at another university. But I didn't, largely because I do not look backward. Looking forward, the practice gave me something that I had not been able to find elsewhere.

Working with hypnotherapy clients, we do not let them off the hook with, "I do not want…" Rather, we compel them to consider what they *do* want. 'What I don't want' creates a vacuum. 'What I want' fills the vacuum.

'What I don't want' is a good place to start because most people do not yet know what they want. The following exercise engages creative brainstorming to transmute from Elimination (What I don't want) to Action (What I do want). Make sure each pairing is relevant to each other.

From Elimination to Action

Engaging in fulltime hypnotherapy practice is a significant change for most people. You are likely reading this book because you have come to the conclusion there are probably some things you need to know that you do not know right now. As you plan and budget your practice, you might begin by thinking about aspects of prior employment that turned you off or that did not resonate with your soul. These are easy because the brain defaults to the negative. Put that list under "What I don't want." Then, for each item on that list, consider a positive alternative, "What I do want is…"

Some items will influence your budget considerations. Others will only influence your style of practice. But both are critical to the happiness and fulfillment you will experience from fulltime practice.

What I don't want	What I do want

My own example

The thing that caused me to move away from the academic environment was that, as department chair, I felt like a bird in a cage. I was expected to do things that required access to resources outside the bars of the cage. Yet there was no key to provide access outside the cage door. It was a middle-management position that demanded creativity, yet I had no freedom or authority to express that creativity.

There was a lot of responsibility, but not enough authority to change anything. The sense of confinement and restraint I felt in that position did not sit well with my soul.

If I were a client in hypnotherapy at that time I may have complained, "I don't want to be told what to do when I know it is not the right thing to do."

"What I *do* want is creative freedom."

And that means... "I want to be able to express my creative energies in a way I see fit. I want to be able to do **my** work the way I want it done."

I could not fly within the confines of the cage, of the institution. There were too many rules to follow, reports to file, and meetings and discussions over what should have been non-issues.

"I don't want to waste life and energy conducting a committee meeting just to move a piece of furniture."

"I do want to work in an environment where my judgment is trusted."

Decide what you want and claim it

Many people sail into business in a wishy-washy sort of way. That is not the path to 6 figures. If you do not know what you want, then it doesn't matter what you get. If you want to be successful, you have to decide, with force and clarity, that you **are** successful. You must claim it.

You have come this far into the book, it is apparent success matters to you. Money matters. Meaning matters even more. So now you make a choice and do something about it. This book is about new beginnings wherever you are.

That is what I do with clients who contract me for *business advisory*, we work from the inside out.

Develop a relationship with money

You would be surprised how many people I work with, when I ask, "What do you need to bring in each month?" they have no clue. They know how to pay bills. They do not know how to generate money.

They do not have a positive relationship with money. An acquaintance wanted to get her professional practice started but she hated money. The result was no matter how much money she earned, she did not get to keep it. Circumstances always prevailed to keep her in debt.

Ambivalence = Poverty

What you want out of your hypnotherapy practice? Or, as you might ask a client, "What do you want out of this life?" The client says she wants to be happy. *You* say you want to be successful. The follow-up question is, of course, "What will it take for you to be happy/successful?"

The most common answers are, "I don't know," and "I want everything." That translates to *nothing*.

So, the appropriate follow-up probe is, "Describe three things that you would have if you were very happy/successful. What are three things you need to feel happy-for-yourself / successful-as-a-hypnotherapist?"

In other words, happiness and success are vague concepts. In order to achieve it, you have to start breaking it down to simple and concrete terms in order to understand what it *is*. Only then can you begin to strategize a means to get there.

It comes down to self-knowledge. You picked up this book because you want to be a successful hypnotherapist. If all you do is read this book, you will only get about one inch closer to that goal (that's the thickness of this book). The rubber hits the road when you put this book down and take stock of your skill level. What do you *need* to get to the skill level you would like? What are you lacking in your confidence to practice?

What do you need to do to overcome ambivalence? How do you convince yourself that poverty is a state of mind in which you assume you deserve nothing better?

Once you decide you are worthy and capable of achieving success, that you are already on the path to having enough and being happy, the rest is simply numbers. Numbers are very easy to work with, because you ascribe meaning to the numbers. One million dollars will make some people ecstatic. One million dollars could make other people miserable because their neighbor has one dollar more.

Chapter Review

We live in a culture of pleasure and excess. That is good for hypnotherapists because such a culture is built on fear. It is a culture that exaggerates the value of money and things. It distorts values and misleads the unwary into desperate circumstances such as debt and poor health. It leads to ambivalence wherein success is deemed achievable only by good fortune.

You cannot counter that culture if you subscribe to it yourself. You cannot overcome fears you share with clients; it makes it too easy to jump in the pit with them.

Knowledge is power. As you increase your knowledge of business finance and start to value the contribution you make to clients' lives, your confidence and credibility will attract clients to you. Only then can you truly 'feel' successful.

Chapter 4 - What is in it for your client?
What value do you hope to give to your clients?

I am often asked how I determine my client fees. I believe that, rather than deciding what you are going to ask for yourself, you need to imagine yourself as the client. What is a session worth to you-the-client? What would you be willing to pay for a session?

That is where conventional thinking stops. It is not just a matter of money (assigning a financial value to the session), it is also a matter of self-worth. The client who says, "I can't afford it," actually conveys a deeper sense of her own self-worth, "I am not worthy of spending this money on myself."

Clearly the purpose of hypnotherapy is to help solve a problem. So instead of trying to *sell* your services, it is more effective to create an opportunity for the client to engage. Discuss the client's needs. "What is your main concern?" A client will often bring up a variety of problems. Let them vent for a while, then ask a couple pointed questions to help them focus. "What is one thing, assuming you can only do one thing, to help you get out of your current situation? What is one thing you would like to see changed?"

That line of questioning helps the client figure out and imagine what her life could be if she did not have this problem. This is the beginning of helping the client build value. "How would not having this problem anymore, when I can help you get there, add value to your life?" "How would your life be different if you did not stutter?" "How would your life be different if you did not smoke?" "How would your life be different if you lost fifty pounds?" The client needs to be able to imagine an alternate reality, what her life would be like minus the issue. If you can help the client imagine that, she will be able to place a value on it herself.

The ensuing conversation solidifies that personal value. "Imagine that you no longer smoke; instead, you identify yourself as a non-smoker." "Imagine that you no longer stutter, but speak fluently with confidence." "Imagine yourself without stage fright, able to appear on stage and deliver a presentation to an audience with confidence." "What is that worth?"

Only then is it time to talk about fees. By the time that question arises in a way you are ready to respond to it, the client has learned the value of the process. The challenge is to reduce the emphasis on money (how much hypnotherapy costs) and redirect it to the opportunity for the client to regain self-worth (specific benefits of positive change).

> I once had an office next door to a pulmonary specialist, a lung doctor. One day he asked that I come to his office to talk with a patient who needed to quit smoking. The patient's first question was how much I charged. Instead of answering immediately, I asked how much he smoked. He gave me a number and I brought out a calculator. I calculated the cost of the cigarettes he smoked in a year's time.
>
> "This time next year, if you come to see me and become a non-smoker, you would have saved the $$$ you normally spend on cigarettes because you no longer smoke. Considering your age, multiply that times ten, because you are adding years to your life. That is instant monetary value. And, assuming you remain healthy from not smoking, imagine doing some things you want to do, such as attending your grandson's high school graduation. How much is that worth to you?"

Establishing value in that way makes the upfront fee less daunting. But make sure you are attending to the correct convincer in that story. The fee is probably a fraction of what he would spend on future cigarettes; but the assurance of witnessing a significant family event strikes an emotional chord that cannot be measured in dollars.

Educate. Educate. Educate.

Realtors tell you the key to their business is Location, Location, Location. If you want to sell hypnotherapy services the key is to Educate, Educate, Educate. Not long, pedantic and boring (like a stereotypical teacher), but quick, relevant and interesting (like a TED talk).

> Many times when meeting new people it comes out that I am a hypnotherapist and they say, "Wow, hypnotherapy, I really need that." So I ask questions like, "What do you need it for?" Or "How do you know hypnotherapy might help you?" In other words, are they serious or just making conversation? In most cases they are simply curious but don't know exactly what question to ask; like the seven-year-old who asks, "Daddy, where do babies come from?"

Do not make any assumptions. Most people have heard of hypnosis and think they know what it is. Their ideas and assumptions reflect surface knowledge. On these impromptu occasions you have only a few minutes to barely scratch that surface. So probe a bit before answering to find out what they really need to know.

> I once found myself sitting beside an actual rocket scientist on an airplane. It was one of the more fascinating conversations in my life. He didn't regale me with the intricacies of jet propulsion. Rather, he described broad principles I could easily understand and yet find fascinating.

To get more information, ask what they know about hypnosis or hypnotherapy. Have they known someone who participated in a stage show? Have they known someone helped by hypnotherapy? If so, what issue was addressed and did that person find it helpful or lasting?

> I have a postcard I hand out as a business card. It is designed to briefly summarize the work I do. That is where the real education begins. The recipient can immediately see that what I do contradicts some of their assumptions. That segues into a description of the types of issues I deal with. Knowing that our time together will likely be short, I direct them to my look at my website when they get home. Upon reading something of interest, I suggest they call me.

A website is crucial, particularly for clients who have a vague interest to begin with. The goal is to further convince them that hypnotherapy works. By the time they pick up the phone, they should be ready to schedule an appointment.

As the conversation continues ask your new acquaintance what their needs might be. By that time you should have exchanged business cards. Though many default to smoking and weight loss, it doesn't take long to figure out that the surface issues represent something more substantive.

- I want to restore balance in my life.
- "Something" (fill in the blank) is not working well in my life.
- I deal with chronic pain.
- I am looking for success in "an area of growth" (fill in the blank)
- Something is missing in my life. Or, I am stuck.
- I "eat / drink / get angry" (fill in the blank) too much and know I need to reduce it.

- My doctor has recommended hypnotherapy for _____.

    Whatever the issue, I can usually cite a success story. For example...

    [The hook] My last weight loss client lost 73 pounds but we didn't talk about dieting at all.

    [Then I explain how it works.] Instead of doing the nutritionist thing—which I did at one time as a clinical nutritionist—I find most people are intelligent. In their own creative intelligence they already know the energy equation; that excess weight happens in the body when you put in more than you take out.

    [I reinforce the simplicity of the process—to which the client has already responded with a grin and nod—with a conspiratorial joke.] If they don't understand that very simple equation, I can usually explain it in about two minutes.

    [Having brought the client into my confidence, I continue with the notion that they can easily experience success with hypnotherapy.] Knowing the energy equation or, for that fact, anything at all about weight management, does not change a person's behavior at all. What really produces change is to work on how you *feel*. Instead of spending a lot of time teaching you what to eat and how to eat, I work out what is eating you, what prevents you from being your knowledgeable self and acting on it. I help you remove the barriers that prevent you from being your best self. [Most people get it.]

Case stories are very important. It's pretty easy to relate them without identifying clients. The point is to emphasize that the process works for people in a variety of circumstances. And many case stories can be told very quickly.

[Case story] One client told me she would drive by a local park, watch the joggers, and wish she could do that. Minus fifty pounds a year later she was preparing for a 10K run. "I never imagined I could join people in a 10K run." For her, that was value.

What value can you deliver right now?

You are reading this book because you want to be a successful hypnotherapist. In the last chapter I asked you to examine your skills and abilities; what can you do with the skills you have right now? What have you been trained to do? The typical person emerging from a hypnotherapy training program should be able to do very simple things like smoking cessation, weight loss, and getting over phobias and fears. You may also have some specialized training; pain management, stress management.

Now you need to start thinking about how you will convert those skills into a value for clients.

Pull out a piece of paper and inventory the skills you have that are of value to potential clients.
This should be a list of everything you can do, but you would not put the entire list in your marketing materials or website. That tends to limit you. (More on that later.)

The idea here is to help you identify the type of people you can help, the types of situations you can deal with. Another purpose is to help you target your audience for speaking and presentation topics.

Many people are unsuccessful early in their practice because they are overwhelmed by the number of things *hypnotherapy* can be used for, as opposed to the things *you* are comfortable doing. So, in this early step, write down only the things you are genuinely comfortable with. You go after those initially. Success at them will help build your confidence, knowing for certain that you can do them.

If you have only recently completed your training, it is okay to have only a very short list. For example, begin with three things. From those three you will grow to six.

In terms of giving value to the client, this self-assessment is imperative. Identifying the skills you have and are capable of doing well creates your initial menu of services. As you write copy for your promotional materials and website, consider limiting the menu to 3-5 things.

List three things you have confidence you can do really well right now in your practice. Then add three things you would like to add within a certain period of time. And then three more things you will add long term. That gives you a plan for growing your business by growing your expertise and confidence level in the process. By picking the things you already know and have confidence in, and doing them, it builds confidence and momentum.

	What are you confident to do right now?	
1.		
2.		
3.		

	What new competencies will you develop in the short term?	By when?
4.		
5.		
6.		

	What new competencies will you develop in the long term?	By when?
7.		
8.		
9.		

Too many people emerge from hypnotherapy training thinking they can do everything, but really they cannot. They have seen a lot of demonstrations but have no clinical experience. Therefore they lack the confidence to practice, which is actually a good thing because it means they have a strong moral compass. If they don't feel good about what they're doing, they also won't be comfortable charging a respectable fee.

For anyone falling into that category—new from a clinical program and not having a lot of clinical experience—it is a good idea to find a clinical supervisor. Go work with someone or hire a clinical coach. Advisory consultation allows you to gradually grow your skills.

Part of Gil Boyne's unconventional education was that he did exactly that. When a new client presented an interesting issue, he would find out as much as he could about that issue. He didn't guess or rely on trial-and-error, he went out and made himself educated.

> I did a lot of that in my own practice. I read most of 1,800 pages of Milton Erickson's case notes. It was very useful. After booking a client for a specific issue I would look through my notes, Milton Erickson's materials, and other books, to find out how others had dealt with it. I didn't necessarily need their scripts, nor did I do exactly what they did, but it gave me a background from which to draw options.

When working in trance with the client you never know what is going to come out, but if you have a closet of experiences to draw from you will be more effective. The ability to 'deal with what emerges' expands as your expertise grows. And you can only grow your expertise through first-hand experience. That's why it is called a practice. The more classes you go to, the more experience you gather, the more skills you are exposed to; the more effective job you can do for clients and the wider range of issues you will feel comfortable addressing.

So, when assembling your initial comprehensive menu of services, make it for yourself, not to be advertised. If someone comes in and asks for something not on the *advertised* list, you have the opportunity to say yes or no. If you say yes, you are going to base your work on what you have already done with other issues. That basic confidence also allows you the option to research that topic and educate yourself so that you are prepared to deal effectively with it.

Continuous learning and improvement

Proficiency in practice requires that you engage in continuous learning and improvement. Continuously hone your skills. It is a nonstop process. Unsuccessful hypnotherapists look at the framed certificate—their 'piece of paper'—hanging on the wall and consider the learning process complete. It's not. In a way, certification does little more than point you in a direction of what you really need to know; things you can only learn with practice and experience. That makes certification only the beginning.

Learning occurs through multiple sources; master classes (both face-to-face and online), books, YouTube videos, DVDs, and conversations with knowledgeable colleagues. Such conversations are most valuable in person, but can also be conducted via social media. *Hypnothoughts.com* and IMDHA/IACT offer forums in which members can discuss any number of topics. Yes, all that learning is time-consuming, but it is critical in order to give value to your clients.

If that is not enough, expand your focus beyond hypnotherapy.

Yes, I have a high level of skill applying the tools I learned in my initial hypnotherapy training. But the thing that allows me to demand a respectable fee is that I have extended my reach beyond hypnotherapy to become a student of the human condition. I study the nature of people. For example, a few things I do that contribute to my work without being hypnosis-oriented...

- I became a trained Mediator and have served on the board of the Tarrant County (TX) Association of Mediators.
- I joined the Fort Worth Area Association for Marriage & Family Therapists. Some members were initially leery about hypnotherapy, but I now speak to the group about once a year.
- I have studied Feng Shui, Dowsing, Energy Medicine, and Qigong; each thru a variety of master teachers.
- I am not ashamed to admit being a Netflix binge-viewer. I latch onto serial programming as varied as British murder mysteries to Food Network elimination contests and TED talks. Not only do I learn about different occupations, I observe how people respond to stress.

I am *always* learning, drawing parallels to hypnotherapy, things that put me in a position to help clients. If you are uncomfortable with that level of single-minded focus, it may be challenging to aspire to a 6 figure practice. There are two things that allow me to devote my energies so completely without disturbing the balance between my work and personal life. 1) I am not just committed to the work; I love doing it. 2) I have a spouse who supports me in my work.

Proficiency in practice requires that you are constantly accumulating experience. Early in practice that means getting out there and *doing it*, whether or not you are confident. The only way to gain confidence is to *do it*; to make mistakes, to recover and do it over again. Over time it gets easier and confidence grows.

> I complain that, early in my practice, I sometimes attracted clients who could not or did not pay. Over time I learned to attract better clients. But the 'bad' client experience was not wasted; I was actively doing hypnotherapy, accumulating experience, uncovering my evolving skill set, adjusting and revising my approach to practice.

The larger your landscape of skills the more effective you can be. There is no shortcut around it.

Chapter Review

Unless it has been recommended by a personal physician, few people realize the value of hypnotherapy. Even when they spontaneously say, "I really need that," it is rarely in earnest. It does, however, express curiosity. To avoid any association with hucksterism it is critical at that point *not* to sell, but rather to educate and create an opportunity for them to engage. Present hypnotherapy as a serious profession and an effective modality. By all means, have fun and emphasize your own skills. That is why it is so important to identify them for yourself. When asked, you want to be able to describe your skills succinctly and with confidence.

Chapter 5 - Who is your client?
Make a good first impression if you want to make a second impression

Who will be attracted to you?
You draw into your practice clients who are similar to you. A client identifies with *you*; your appearance, your lifestyle, your social economic status. Believe it or not, you put out signals that attract such clients. Though such signals are superficial, it supports the admonition, "You only get one chance to make a first impression."

At a bit deeper level, it sometimes helps to have 'walked the talk', so a client assumes you are able to help them with similar problems. Such things might be revealed in your elevator speech or somewhere on your website.

On the other hand, a well-known colleague had an alcoholic father who beat him as a child. He never resolved that issue himself, so he would not work with alcoholics. He found he could not be objective when faced with an alcoholic client. Since that meant not being able to give his best work, he refused to work with alcoholics.

It is important you set such limits on service in your own mind; but emphasize *positives* in your promotions. Obviously any issue you prefer not to address will be omitted from your menu of services. If a potential client inquires about such an issue, simply and graciously refer him to someone else.

Personal choices are derived from self-knowledge. In the prior chapter you listed the areas of work you are most comfortable with. Here, what areas are you not comfortable with? In contrast to a lack of confidence in your skills; in what areas might you lack objectivity?

The choice is an ethical decision to give your best work to your clients. Ask yourself...

> Can I look at a client with respect? (e.g., You cannot face clients who abuse alcohol or drug abuse because you have suffered under others with addiction issues.)
> Can I help the client without jumping into the pit? (e.g., You have been a victim of rape or incest yourself and therefore identify too closely with the client's suffering.)
> Is the client struggling with an issue I have not resolved for myself? (e.g., You are contracted to help a client lose weight or stop smoking and you are overweight or smoke.)

Make your client a mirror of you

Who would consent to paying hundreds of dollars for sessions that take place in an office that is noisy, dirty and shabby; in a dodgy neighborhood or building? Low rent is convenient, but translates to low fees. Neither should you go into debt to set up a posh office environment. The key is to strike a balance.

> My first couple offices were in small complexes inhabited by independent professionals such as myself; dentists, accountants, psychology-oriented therapists, etc. The buildings were attractive, but the interiors were dated. A new coat of paint and a thorough cleaning created a palette for relevant wall coverings and comfortable furniture. I owned the first office, so I could do what I wanted. I rented the next office; but made sure the landlord first agreed to the renovations I needed.
>
> I do not target 'rich' clients, but I want any such client to feel comfortable in my space. For clients of lesser means, who find it a struggle to pay my fee; I don't want them to feel like they are paying for my affluence; rather the

environment has to support my credibility as a successful practitioner.

I tell the success stories of prior clients to a current client as she sits on a $5,000 Chesterfield couch. Further reinforcement is conveyed by framed certificates on walls that are painted in Feng Shui-selected colors.

She is not just comfortable paying my fee. The entire effect, including the fee, convinces her of her imminent success in resolving whatever issue brought her to me.

Now, don't overdo it. You do not need a $3,000 Armani suit to impress clients (and I did not pay $5,000 for my couch, I bought it from a friend who did). You have to come across as being comfortable with yourself. You don't want to be cheap, but you want to look professional; clean and proficient. Again, it is less about *you* and **all about the client**.

Pictures on the wall, paint colors, flooring, furniture, lighting; everything in your office space contributes to professionalism and branding.

How would you like to be seen? If you want to command a fee commensurate with a doctor, lawyer or psychiatrist, you have to present yourself (and your office) in a way that matches the fee. Take a look in the mirror; is that what you see?

Behavior set

It goes without saying that a professional is proficient at what she professes to do. The difficulty is in proving it; not just to the client, but to yourself as well. One reason for taking inventory of your skills in the prior chapter is to remind yourself of what you *can* do. If that inventory is an honest account of your skills, you need only look at your menu of services to remind yourself you know how to practice effectively.

A potential client, on the other hand, is guided strictly by perception. To be perceived as a professional, start with your personal habits. Give up the notion of personal preferences. A successful hypnotherapy practice is less about **you** and **all about the client**. Stop me if you have heard this before; **You don't get a second chance to make a first impression!**

> **Manner**: Friendly yet authoritative vs. any extreme between haughty and insecure
> **Personal conduct**: Erect posture and eye contact vs. slouch and shifty eyes
> **Language choice**: Professional yet accessible vs. overly familiar and crude
> **Attire**: Clean and pressed vs. any extreme between flashy and dirty
> **Office environment**: Organized and inviting vs. Haphazard

I make extensive recommendations during live trainings, more so than is appropriate for this book. Bottom line, my students are prone to resisting my recommendations. As they express the notion, "That's just not *me*," I remind them, "A successful hypnotherapy practice is less about *you* and *all about the client*. You don't get a second chance to make a first impression!" That first impression must convince the *potential* client to give you a chance.

The first impression is in your person. Next is how you talk and communicate. That is followed by your promotional materials (business card, brochures, website). Finally, you want to reinforce any and all positive impressions with your office. Actually, these can happen in any order. This order is most common when you are getting yourself *out there*, meeting people in public.

To receive the success this book advocates for you, you must appeal to clients with the resources to pay the fee you want. If you project airy-faery, tie-died mysticism (i.e., poor and unprofessional), people with the means will not make a donation to your individualism.

Personal hygiene is another sensitive, but critical, issue. Hypnotherapists work in close physical proximity with clients. You obviously do not want body odor, but neither should you reek of perfume or cologne. Be aware of halitosis (bad breath). Brush your teeth before you meet with a new client. Better yet, rinse with mouthwash and pop a breath mint to be sure. Nothing puts off a client more than the distraction of questionable hygiene.

Attire

With some clients, you have to be cautious not to overdress in a way that makes the client uncomfortable. You need not be dressed exactly like your clients; they may be dressed either better or worse. The key is to strike a balance that maintains professional respect, so they willingly pay your fee and engage your services.

> On occasion I counsel clients on their financial health. My attire is comfortable and attractive without being 'rich'. This reinforces the notion that my fee is consistent with the expertise I demonstrate in my work, not just an opportunity to enrich myself at the client's expense.

To some extent, professional attire becomes your uniform; and, as a self-employed person you cannot afford to be caught out of uniform. You never know where you might meet a client. So, every day as you leave your bedroom to face the world, you need to be dressed and pressed. Whether you have a client or not, you are on the clock. Dressing ready-to-work is a mark of respect for your clients as well as for yourself.

That is a particular need in this profession. One should not be continuously trolling for clients, but you never know where and when you might meet the next one. Repeat, it is your responsibility to look, dress and behave professionally at all times. If you are not prepared to make that commitment, put this book back on the shelf.

Competition

When starting a new practice, the first thing you want to know is if there are people like you doing work like you. People in marketing and business think in terms of competition. It is more helpful to think of it as knowing your professional community.

If your town is laden with a hypnotherapist on every corner, that doesn't mean you will have a hard time making your business successful. It could mean there is a strong demand for hypnotherapists. Whatever it means, it is a good idea to get to know your colleagues and find common ground for collaboration.

> I attended a Chamber of Commerce meeting in a small town near me where there were twenty-one chiropractors. You might imagine everyone in town had a bad back. Yet somehow there is enough business to sustain them all. In the eight years since, I have seen only a few of them go out of business. That indicates there must be a demand for their service.

In addition to knowing who else in your area is doing hypnotherapy, find out how they position themselves, what type of fees they charge, and what type of clients they work with. Basic information can come from the phonebook, or

Googling keywords relevant to your own specialties. Websites often include hours, fees, and details on how they conduct their work. You might also call as a potential client, just to see how they do business.

After locating your peers and exploring how they work, you can decide for yourself whether you are going to be like them, undercut them, or set yourself and your services apart from them. That is a choice you make for yourself.

That is another reason why it is so important to know yourself and know your skills. Know what you can do at this moment and how you want to expand on your current skill set. Then make a plan to go learn the new skills.

Beyond knowing who your competition is, get to know them as peers. Seek to establish collaborative relationships with them. Competition usually arises from fear that either you or they will get a client's business. It is a zero sum calculation. Whereas in collaboration, you agree to refer clients who will benefit from each other's specialties. Or you might explore how to work together to help each other grow, but also to make hypnotherapy a respectable profession in your market.

All successful marketing is niche marketing. It is important to decide whom to serve. There is only so much one person can do in the course of a day or week. So you have to select issues you are going to concentrate your efforts on. A marketing campaign that claims you can save everyone ends up serving nobody. The implication is that you have no clue what you're doing or who you want to work with.

Look at the orchard and pick the low-lying fruit first. Ask yourself what you enjoy doing most in your practice. What makes your heart sing? What age group, gender, etc. are you most comfortable with?

How to set yourself apart from others

Begin with your origin story. That may include your personal experience with hypnotherapy. What in your life resonated with hypnotherapy? If you have been helped by hypnotherapy yourself, that is a good place to start.

> I came to hypnotherapy not knowing what it was; but the concept clicked for me. It aligned with things I had been doing as a health educator and health scientist. I immediately saw the congruency. As a student of hypnotherapy, I was impressed that it worked so well. It expanded my identity by growing my competencies. As I explain it to clients, "I am still a health educator, but I added a very effective new tool to my belt."

To be unique as a hypnotherapist, return to the section on self-knowledge. First look at your skill set, your competencies, within and outside hypnotherapy. If you are starting it as a new career, what was your prior career? And what in that, and perhaps other career experiences, can you bring to bear that will help you carve out a unique niche in hypnotherapy?

> I have known quite a number of substance abuse counselors who entered that field after recovering from their own experience as an abuser. Someone who has been helped to overcome alcohol addiction may use that first-hand experience to help others with similar addictions. They have a unique understanding of the struggles one goes through in that situation. Hypnotherapists with that background are likely to attract into their practice clients who are like what they used to be.

It is imperative that your origin story be authentic, *your* story. For example...

Recovered academic

I describe myself as a "recovered academic." It informs a client that I had once been an academic. In order to be an academic I had to accumulate years and years of schooling to earn a doctorate, to become a professor and a content specialist in my field.

The *recovered* part means I no longer work in the academic environment. While an academic I experienced a lot of struggles and challenges. I freed myself from that; from working within tight constraints and not having the creative freedom to do things I really wanted to do. There were things I could not do while serving an institution that now I can. I phrase it as, "I broke loose from the University to what I call the Universe-city, my school without walls."

In that respect the *recovered academic* label draws a certain type of client to my practice. I share a common experience with people who currently feel trapped in their job. I know what it means to feel like you have no power or freedom to be your creative self. Yes, I was an academic, but the relevant parallel most people draw is the idea of feeling confined and trapped in a job doing work that does not feed their soul. They work very hard to make a lot of money and have nothing to show for it. Or they spend their time making hard-earned money at the expense of time stolen from life and family. They acquire material things to impress people they don't even like.

The notion of being a recovered academic is almost the same as saying I am a recovered worker bee, doing things I did not like to do, and not having opportunities to do things I truly wanted to do. As a university professor I had freedom in many ways. I loved being a professor. I loved to teach. It was only when I became an academic administrator that I felt confined. I felt trapped. I felt I was expected to fly, but they had just cut my wings. I was given tasks I could not complete because I was not given relevant resources as well. With that realization, as well as the desire for a new challenge, I left.

When I share with clients the sense of freedom to be me, it is so exhilarating. That is what *they* want. That is the value I will add to their lives, as I help free them from their own shackles; shackles they have created for themselves, either from a job or a life situation, a marriage or other relationship, anything that confines them. I liberate them.

Recovery story

> When I consider what it is I offer clients, I specifically avoid using the term *hope*; though many of my clients interpret it as hope. I prefer to think I offer a living solution (my personal example) to a problem they can identify with. "My problem is not identical to yours, but you can draw enough from it in the similarities to know this is exactly where you are stuck. I have been where you have been, and I am living proof that there is a solution in sight, and I can show you how."

Make yourself unique

Every person who chooses to become a hypnotherapist has a unique story. You just have to find it. No one just wakes up one morning and declares they want to be a hypnotherapist. Somehow you were led by forces known, or unknown, onto this path.

As you are preparing to deplane, a flight attendant comes on the intercom and says, "Thank you for flying with American Airlines. We know you have many options to fly to Dallas, but you chose us and we appreciate it." You chose hypnotherapy. Presumably, you had a reason.

> In my university days, I asked students under my advisement how they ended up in their current major. Responses varied from "I don't know" or "It was convenient" to "My parents forced me into it." Very few cited personal conviction. Such ambivalence created more interest in good grades than in learning something of value to their eventual career.
>
> As a brief aside, I have encountered numerous 'certification junkies' in hypnotherapy with a similar mindset. They accumulate training hours and certifications that add to the alphabet soup after their name, but in the process do not develop expertise. In essence, they have collected a massive reservoir of information but cannot practice.

The program FOOD NETWORK STAR requires contestants to convey a POV (Point of View). That POV, if they win the competition and are rewarded with their own Food Network program, is what they will use to appeal to viewers. Business publications use USP (Unique Selling Point) for a similar purpose. Whether POV or USP, the presumption is that you have under 30 seconds to make your case. Can you do it?

Certification as a piece of paper or building a skill

Whether you make your case as a POV, USP or elevator speech, do not waste precious time mentioning certification or your organization membership. Those are characteristics expected of all professionals, so they do not set you apart. The hypnotherapy school you attended or instructor you studied under is even more obscure. Save all that for conversations with other hypnotherapists.

Instead, emphasize your specialization, or maybe a unique approach. Describe the approach, not the name you have given it. In other words, anything that a potential client cannot immediately understand without a definition or explanation, leave it out. That includes jargon, acronyms, theory and personalities.

To be clear, it is not ethical to practice with zero certification, and membership in one or more professional organizations is critically important. During your training you probably heard about a variety of membership opportunities, comparing and contrasting organizations. Those distinctions are important to you as a hypnotherapist, but not to potential clients.

Since there is no standardized curriculum for hypnotherapy, professional organizations such as ACHE, IMDHA, IACT, NGH, and ICBCH each have their own set of standards. This is not necessarily good for the field. Further, too many students accept the certificate of completion as some type of end, rather than as a means to an end. They expend the requisite dollars and hours to merely get their piece of paper.

That is what makes the mention of certification in the elevator speech irrelevant. The implications of 'Certification' are meaningful only to someone already in-the-know. It is preferable to describe skills that should be relevant to a potential client. Of course that is much more difficult. It is easier to think in terms of I, I, I. But to create relevance and value for the potential client, replace I, I, I with you, you, you. For example, "'I' am certified" vs. "This is a hypnotherapy skill that can help 'you'."

Having acquired the piece of paper, your certification may support your professional status, but it does not define you, i.e., just because the certificate names you Clinical Hypnotherapist, if you lack the actual skills or confidence in those skills, the certificate is a lie. Even if you have the skills and confidence, an active practice requires that you maintain and grow those abilities.

Even though training is delivered by approved instructors, based on an approved curriculum, and capped off with an approved test, few training programs do adequate skills testing. A certificate indicates little more than that one attended the course. The lack of a rigorous clinical practicum means some students do the 'required' homework, while many do not. It really does not matter how many hundreds of hours a school requires if the certificate is rubber-stamped without some assurance that the student can actually *do* something.

Chapter Review

When it comes right down to it, hypnotherapy is a people business. Most clients are stepping outside their comfort zone to engage in hypnosis. Your very presence has to convince them they are making a good decision.

As much as you might like to think you are selling a product (a specific program you implement), the real product is you. You learn in basic training to convince clients of the efficacy of hypnotherapy, so they can relax and experience the benefits. But the bigger challenge is to get clients to part with their money. That requires you to exude competence and confidence.

Throughout this book you are encouraged to engage in continuous learning. The obvious inference is hypnotherapy skills. However, in order to raise your fees to a level commensurate with earning 6 figures, you really need to get to know yourself.

Chapter 6 - Who are your peers?
How do you position yourself (in hypnotherapy)?

> Hypnotherapist: *What can I help you with today?*
> Client: *My life is terrible. I just have no confidence. Can you help me find confidence?*
> Hypnotherapist: *What if I tell you that you have tons of confidence? You have tons of confidence that you will fail. Would you like me to help you park all that confidence in the right place?*

If you want to be successful, associate with people who are successful. Then do what they do. That may mean some type of apprenticeship or developing a mentor relationship. Either way, associate with master practitioners who serve as 'aspirational' peers, people you want to be like someday; people in whose presence your confidence grows in a positive direction.

Then consider not just what they are doing now as successful practitioners, but how they got there. In hypnotherapy you cannot just DO what someone else is doing and hope it produces the same success. In hypnotherapy, the DOING is not all that difficult or complex. Rather, what creates success is wisdom; which is the creative use of knowledge.

In other words, learning occurs with a range of qualities that determine what we are able to do with knowledge once it has been acquired. Bloom's Taxonomy of Learning is a standard of Educational Psychology that describes those qualities. Briefly...

- *Knowledge*: As the bottom tier, Knowledge refers merely to the acquisition of facts. If you can remember information and facts given to you, you have knowledge. In hypnotherapy training, you have learned enough to pass a multiple choice exam.
- *Comprehension*: A parrot can be said to have knowledge, since it repeats what it hears; but it has no understanding of what it means. Comprehension is the ability to understand something, to explain its meaning in your own words. In hypnotherapy, you have learned enough to pass an exam comprised mainly of short answer questions. To determine true comprehension, the questions use slightly different contexts that when the information was originally received.
- *Application*: This is the ability to use information for a practical purpose. In hypnotherapy training, let's say you know the language and sequence of trance induction. A clinical exam at the Application level would ask you to demonstrate a trance induction following those principles.
- *Analysis:* This is critical thinking, the ability to break things down. In hypnotherapy training, why do some instructors recommend that you count downward (say, from 5 to 1) on the induction and count upward (say, from 1 to 5) on the trance termination? More importantly, how do you apply the same reasoning in the middle of a trance session? It is problem-solving at a level of using what you already know.
- *Synthesis*: At this level you create new information. During a clinical exam, a hypnosis subject goes into abreaction. You have been trained specifically how to cope with the abreaction, but each client abreacts to their own specific emotional triggers, and no hypnotherapist can ever hope to know what they all might be. Synthesis is the part where

you invent a way to help the client through their unique emotional experience.

- *Evaluation*: At the highest level of learning, you can use Evaluation to reflect and recalibrate your own work, or you might use some combination of Application, Analysis and Synthesis to evaluate the work of others. To evaluate the abreaction experience previously described, in a clinical training setting the supervisor would provide qualitative feedback; not just what you did, but how the things you did impacted the session and client experience. As you subsequently become established in your own practice, you can eventually apply self-reflection for the same purpose.

Learning should be a process of cultivating wisdom. It occurs both formally and informally, from great teachers but also from not-so-great teachers. From some occasions you learn what to do, from others you learn what not to do.

> I was studying Feng Shui under Grandmaster Lin Yun (Lin Rinpoche). There was a special ceremony at the chapel in the seminary school at Harvard University. Students filed up to the stage to be *enlightened* by the teacher as he tapped our forehead to open the 'third eye'. My friends were afraid of what might happen, so they pushed me forward as the guinea pig. I had no idea what was going to happen. I arrived onstage and stood before Rinpoche. He looked directly into my eyes and intoned, "Some teachers require that you have only the one teacher, but this teacher requires you to have as many teachers as your life requires you to have."
>
> In that same instant he tapped my forehead. A bolt of electricity coursed through my body. All I remember was the feeling of sublime peace, and his kind eyes. I sensed

pure love and a calm I had never experienced. My body buzzed but my mind became like the still surface on a lake; still, yet alive; calm, yet excited. Something magical had transpired and my life would never be the same again.

This level of knowing is beyond Bloom's taxonomy and definitely outside what anyone else has taught me. In the days and years to come, I began to understand that the experience opened a path in my work and life that has helped to dissolve limiting beliefs. I was given the gift of creativity—a freedom to manifest new ideas to help my clients.

Could this be wisdom? This all happened before I came to hypnotherapy. You may not need the touch of an enlightened being to achieve wisdom; but you do need to push yourself to higher levels of learning.

Most hypnotherapy training emphasizes Knowledge and Comprehension, with brief exposure to Application. (Not to worry, that is a major criticism of mainstream education as well.) If you want to do the type of work that allows you to charge a higher fee, you need to learn at the higher levels of Bloom's taxonomy; Analysis, Synthesis and Evaluation. Doing so for long enough puts you on the path to Wisdom—the creative application of knowledge.

> The initial certification training in hypnotherapy was a new experience for me. Throughout all the academic training that preceded my PhD, my classmates had a common background. As an undergraduate student, I was in classes with the same people for several years. My peers in graduate school all came from a similar background that qualified us for a specialized program. The coursework presumed basic knowledge of the field. Evaluation was comprehensive and demanding. Anyone who couldn't hack

it dropped out or failed. There were the inevitable few who skated by with the least acceptable effort. But most of my classmates were more like me academically than not. We understood there was a level of knowledge and practice to be mastered, and we buckled down and did it.

Hypnotherapy training is entirely different. Too often there are no prerequisites of prior training or life experience. Some schools go through the rigor of licensing regulations required by their states, while others operate outside governmental regulation. Professional organizations for hypnotherapy only provide "approval status" for schools while they depend on the integrity of school operators to seek licensure if their states require it.

The only qualifications I needed for my initial hypnotherapy training was the ability to pay the tuition. Everyone in my class cohort finished the training and passed the certification test (though for some it took considerable coaxing and coaching).

Two other students had a master's degree in a professional field. The others did not have even a college education. That is not to say that lack of a formal education would make them inferior practitioners; only that there was wide diversity of professional background.

With that range of diversity in the field of hypnotherapy, where do you want to position your practice? How do you want to be perceived? To be a professional hypnotherapist does not require a PhD. There are many highly effective hypnotherapists who lack that level of formal education, yet have acquired knowledge in other ways. You can also take a trades-person approach. You will deal with simpler issues and can therefore get by on less knowledge, but it is an approach that works for many people.

This book advocates developing the capacity to do deeper work. That is where you can start to increase your fees. But that level of work relies heavily on linguistics. Being articulate and proficient in language work is a critical advantage. It starts with reading; reading widely and deeply. It is enhanced by talking; discussions of what you have read with other widely read people; putting into oral expression the concepts and ideas you are learning. And through talking, you develop fluency, the ability to think on your feet and express yourself clearly.

In a nutshell, that is what one does in graduate school – read, discuss, read some more, ask questions, answer questions, come to conclusions, draw parallels, debate, defend, advocate, explain. It is knowledge-building and problem-solving at its finest. If you want to position yourself in hypnotherapy at the highest level, you have to add all that to your skill set. Even if you have been to graduate school, and particularly if you have not, you need to associate with peers who can help you grow that skill set.

Hypnotist or Hypnotherapist?

Though formal definitions exist, there is little discrimination in certification programs between hypnosis and hypnotherapy. As a matter of practicality, most newly certified graduates are much more competent at hypnosis than hypnotherapy. Of course, most have viewed numerous videotapes of hypnotherapy in practice, but few have had extensive time to practice on their own, and even fewer have done so under close supervision.

Consider that (in Texas) someone seeking to become licensed as a Marriage and Family Therapist (LMFT) must complete 3,000 hours of work experience, with at least 200 hours of direct supervision. That would be equivalent to 33 hours in the context of a 500 hour hypnotherapy training. It is no wonder that new hypnotherapists confidently induce trance, only to get freaked out by an abreaction.

The way to avoid the unforeseeable issues that emerge when working with a therapy client is to engage hypnosis for entertainment. But that presents its own set of problems. Successful stage hypnotists make it look easy, but it requires skill and practice as well. So, therapy vs. entertainment, be prepared for hard work. And just because you can do one does not mean you should attempt the other. You should not try to be everything to everybody.

Some very good hypnotists practice in group settings, traveling from town to town conducting mass sessions to stop smoking or stimulate weight loss. Again, it has the potential to produce good income, but requires specific skills. And heaps of practice.

Most of the colleagues I associate with have an office where they see clients face-to-face, working with individual clients to resolve a variety of issues. Some accompany their session work with hypnotherapy CDs for phobias and anxieties.

I also know hypnotherapists who operate successfully in medical and dental offices.

In fact, while writing this, it occurs to me that hypnotherapy, as a field, has very wide diversity. Not just in how and where one practices, but in the fees charged, anywhere from $50 to $700 a session. So, where do you fit? Where would you *like* to fit? When you can answer that, it is time to start looking for your aspirational peers. Who can you learn from who is already doing it successfully?

In other words, think of how you can grow beyond your initial training. By all means, use what you learned in basic training, but do not be limited by it. You may have to jump in charging a nominal amount by the session. Book paying clients as they come. Schedule pro bono (free) clients to get more practice. Watch your practice evolve to deeper work as you gain experience and confidence. Raise your fee as your level of work improves.

> I have chosen to do work that is therapeutic. In contrast to being entertaining, I am satisfied with being a good host (clients often comment how much they enjoy my sessions). I see clients individually because I want to engage them personally. And, of course, there is the gratification of doing in-depth, life-transforming work; work that changes lives positively.

Chapter Review

However you choose to practice, there is a definite advantage in associating yourself with skilled mentors and coaches. But you also have a responsibility to continuous education and self-cultivation. If you aspire to a 6 figure practice, you must never settle with the status quo. You must constantly look forward to the next challenge, explore novel approaches, develop innovative skills and, of course, grow in positive confidence such that success be yours. Go beyond Bloom's!

Chapter 7 - Fees and practice strategy
Pick an approach

Hypnotherapy training curricula commonly recommend a couple standard ways to set up sessions. Session lengths are usually between an hour or two. Many simple issues can be dealt with in a package of three sessions.

Your fee is largely dependent on how you want to work with your clients. Some of that is determined by your training, in terms of how you were trained to do the work. You may vary your approach over time based on continuing education and accumulation of experience, for which you would be justified in raising your hourly rate.

You may also vary time and fees on different tiers of service. Charge more for services that require special expertise. Basically, there are three different sets of circumstances clients present.

1. Stop suffering. Clients seek to alleviate pain (whether physical, emotional or spiritual). They suffer a specific issue and want out of the misery.
2. Prevent reoccurrence. Clients want permanent relief from suffering, to make sure it never happens again.
3. Seek a better life circumstance. "I want to be happy," which actually translates to #1 or #2 or both.

From that perspective, the depth and permanency of the therapy solution influences the fee you command.

1. Basic hypnotherapy training provides strategies and solutions to stop the suffering. It can often be done in one session but, as noted above, a series of three sessions is most commonly recommended. The first session is usually longer than the other sessions, since that is where you get to know the client and find

out what the issue is. Split any remaining time among the two follow-up sessions.

> Weight Loss programs vary according to the amount of weight to be lost. Obviously it is not realistic to expect to lose 100 pounds in three weeks. There are any number of simple hypnosis strategies to help a client lose weight.

2. To prevent reoccurrence may require more time, since you need to search for an underlying issue. If you do not deal with the underlying issue, a bad habit will simply return later in a new form. This process requires a couple additional sessions, each time 'dealing with what emerges'. The goal is to eliminate a pattern of negative behaviors by transmuting the underlying emotional energy in the subconscious mind.

> To lose weight, it is not about what you are eating, it is about what is eating you.

3. Helping the client achieve a better life circumstance requires that you teach the client how to adapt to her changed life. Even though she has changed, people around her have not; requiring some communication skills. She may also need to modify elements within her home and work environment to eliminate triggers. Obviously, this requires yet more time.

> To support new weight loss habits, practice specifically how you will respond to friends and family who try to sabotage your success.

Strategizing how you will work with clients, based on the above, establishes how much time you are going to engage.

By the hour versus by the program

However you charge, you are selling time. Unless you practice in a way that you can solve a problem in 20 minutes, it may be better that you sell by the session than by the hour.

In my experience, a critical part of effective practice is the process of establishing a deep level of trust in me. Therefore I do not do quickie sessions. I spend a good amount of time interviewing the client and engaging her in the process so she feels ownership of the process.

The way I split up my 20-hour protocol

The iChange Therapy process I designed for my own practice requires that clients commit and pay upfront for what I call "my 20-hour protocol." In a matter of four or five sessions, with session lengths varying according to the client's issues, 20 hours of work gets the client in a pretty good place.

This system works well for me and evolved over a dozen years of practice. My most effective results were occurring within the context of about twenty hours of work. It is most relevant to a certain type of client and I have geared my practice toward that clientele. A long first session gives me the time necessary to get the client 'out of the pit'. The rest of the time is divvied up among follow-up sessions.

The first 'session' is a long day with me, averaging about eight hours (as short as four hours and as long as sixteen). It varies based on the client's availability, my stamina, and intuiting when to start and stop. That last part comes with experience.

In the follow-ups there may be more small pits to dig out of. But I spend most of that time educating the client, teaching new ways to communicate and make decisions. Within a matter of three to five sessions, accumulating twenty hours, the client is pretty ready to go, with the skills to help her stay out of trouble.

So, how much is your time worth?
- How much money do you need? Start with the budget discussed later in this chapter.
- How much you would like to be paid? Perhaps you are replacing income from a prior career. Perhaps you have an idea of the prevailing rate in your marketplace.
- How much do you deserve to be paid? Consider the ways that you are uniquely effective with clients. It may be specialty skills such as Parts Therapy or Past Life Therapy. Or it may simply be that you have built a highly positive reputation.

Can you sell it?
Switch chairs for a moment and pretend you are a client. How much would you-the-client be willing to pay you-the-hypnotherapist to get out of your suffering? What is that worth to you? How much are you worth to yourself?

> Many students in my conference sessions gasp when they hear the fees I charge. My point in revealing it is not to brag, but to suggest you can ask whatever amount you want. Their counterpoint is that the market will only pay what the market can bear. I agree you need to have an objective understanding of the social economics of your clientele. My further point is that my clients are rarely 'rich'; rather, I convince them they are worth the benefits to be derived from working with me; and that I am worth every penny they give me.

Establishing your fee is the easy part, finding clients able and willing to pay is where the tire meets the road. Jumping back a bit, who *are* your clients? Where will they find the money to pay you? *Are* they able to pay you? Are they the kind of people who can see value that is intangible?

Then, how good are you at convincing potential clients of the value they will get from being relieved of their suffering? You have to effectively package your services and offer them to clients in a way that the value is immediately evident.

Ask clients what they think it is worth for them to be able to stop the suffering and also learn a new set of skills so that they don't go back to the same problems in the future.

"What is it worth to you to _____?"
"Can you imagine your life minus the suffering and having the skills to make better choices? What is that worth?"

Oftentimes a client may have gone through years of conventional therapy and not achieved any positive change. And yet hypnotherapy offers an almost immediate solution.

How busy do you want to be?

> I go to a very skilled and experienced hairstylist. She charges a minimal fee and has not raised it in a long time. She is very efficient. I get in-and-out; wash, cut and style in 30 minutes. I love that she is on time and I need not sit and wait. She schedules clients back-to-back, 30 minutes apiece, four days a week. "I love being busy on the days I work, so I schedule back-to-back-to-back. I get my work done quickly and I don't need more clients. With happy, established clients I work four days and play three. I make enough money and am happy."

There is something to be said for contentment and knowing what you want. And, when you get there to know how to relax and enjoy it.

> I am still learning that myself, to enjoy time when I am not busy. I came from a world where I had to be busy, busy, busy all the time. Now I am not so busy because I am

efficient and effective in my work. It is a whole new work model for me.

I have time to play, but it is an area I need to practice, to play when I am not seeing clients; knowing that when I do see clients the work is highly intense. Playtime away from clients replenishes my energies so I am ready to deliver the level of work I know my clients appreciate. My flower garden gives me joy and sweat!

Profit and Loss

Back to brass tacks. It should be evident by now that setting your fee is a multi-faceted exercise.

Variables
- What is your life worth?
- What do you deliver?
- What can your market bear?
- Are you able to attract the kind of clients willing to pay for the value you create for them?
- How many hours a day do you want to work?
- How many days do you want to work?
- What is the amount of revenue you desire for yourself, to support the lifestyle you want?

Fixed costs
- Rent
- Utilities (water, gas, electric, phone, internet)
- Supplies (paper, ink, toilet paper, cleansers)
- Advertising (business cards, brochures, print ads, website host)
- Taxes, Insurance

There is a tendency not to include real and continuous expenses. Most hypnotherapists new to business establish an arbitrary fee; $X.00 per hour. That may reflect what you consider the cost of your time or the value of the service. Either way, it is not an account of your true costs.

You must know what expenses you have at the end of the day. If you bring in $1,000 in client fees, what portion of that do you actually get to put in your pocket? It is not so much what you bring in, it's how much you get to keep.

> For instance, my dentist has multiple leases on expensive equipment and his office suite. He has a staff. He has to pay for things like advertising, liability insurance and so on. When a patient pays $1,000, the dentist gets to keep maybe 10%. 90% goes to expenses. He works very hard, of course, and is well compensated (by his business).
>
> He is not working for himself, he is working for the equipment leasing company and his landlord. To stay in business he has to maintain a consistent money stream that supports his employees. So he bills $10,000 a day but only gets to keep $1,000. Imagine how many easier ways one might make $1,000 and pocket most of it.

In hypnotherapy it is much easier to set up an efficient business practice with minimal expenses. It's easy to imagine that of every dollar in client fees you may get to keep $0.80. That is a better formula for a sustainable business. The key is to keep expenses low.

Pay yourself

It is beyond the scope of this book to discuss the merits of practicing as an individual vs. incorporating your hypnotherapy practice as a business. You might want to consult a Certified

Public Accountant to explore the tax advantages. One way or the other, you need to pay yourself.

One approach is to create a budget for yourself; all expenses and income related to hypnotherapy; with any income above and beyond what you need to make your budget going into your pocket. Another option is to create a budget item to pay yourself a salary; then write yourself a check from a business account set up separate from your household accounts.

When you set up your hypnotherapy practice as a business, the money that comes in is not yours; it belongs to the business; and the business pays you. In a way, you are both boss and employee.

> The reason I bring this up here is that too many people I have addressed at hypnotherapy conferences do not pay themselves. They do not give themselves a paycheck. In many cases it's because they are basically giving away their services. This hurts all of us in the field of hypnotherapy for two reasons. 1) If one charges too little and does poor work, that stains everyone in the field by reinforcing the notion of charlatanism. 2) Even if one does good work, a low fee detracts from professionalism, making it harder for true professionals to demand a respectable fee.

Career-changers, in particular, have a vested interest in making sure that the personal salary is accounted for. Imagine someone making $3,000 a month in take-home pay before quitting his job. That $3,000 a month covered his living expenses. If he makes only 10% profit from his hypnotherapy practice, to take home $3,000 a month requires $30,000 in revenue.

Job vs. Profession
Pay yourself not to *do* hypnotherapy, but as a hypnotherapist. As a hypnotherapist business owner, you set goals to bring in

money to pay for the time you spend accounting, on the phone, convincing clients; your job is not just hypnotherapist in the therapy room, your job is all of the above. You have to account for that time or pay someone to account for it.

> I know people who just practice and pay a business manager. My brother is a physician. He works only as a doctor. He does nothing except doctoring. He pays other people to do all the things that keep his practice alive. Billing is done by a company. He has a business manager. He has a receptionist who takes calls and books appointments for his patients. He owns his building. It is an opportunity cost; he put out a hunk of cash to buy it, but it is income-producing; and one less expense since there is no mortgage to service.

You have to *cost* (verb) everything.

An entrepreneur considers every aspect of the business that contributes to the client walking in the door and writing a check. Everything that contributes to setting client fees has a cost factor. Tangible things are easy to cost, just look at the price tag.

> For example, the clothes you wear. There are outfits I own that I only wear to present at conferences. In my accounting they are charged as an expense. Every mile I drive that is business-related is recorded for tax purposes (as an expense that turns into a write-off).

To cost intangible things requires assigning a value to it. There are more of those things than you might imagine; researching a specific issue prior to working with a client, creating forms, writing articles. Then there is time not actively in front of a client but engaged in client recruitment, such as free presentations that put you in front of potential clients. How much time do you spend at such activities and how do you reward yourself for them?

More concrete, but still intangible (since there is no price tag); bookkeeping, answering the phone, copying & filing; for which there would be a price tag if you paid someone else to do it. And, if you are paying service providers, there are still business meetings [time] to set up and maintain those services.

Then there are the things that involve a combination of cost and time. Paid lectures you attend. Chamber of Commerce (membership $$) functions (meals $$, volunteering [time]).

Attending professional conferences is a significant investment.

> Organization membership
> Conference registration
> Travel (a plane seems more costly than driving until you factor in a cost for time)
> Housing & Meals

Everything you do has a cost factor if it contributes to the business. See time investment as a resource.

> For a long time I chafed at the notion of giving free presentations and attending local functions like Chamber of Commerce meetings; time spent when I was not making any money *right now*. But Steve constantly reminded me that I was my own best advocate; that any time I was in front of people, clients show up.
>
> I know now to turn the equation around. I put that expenditure of time in my advertising budget. 1) The money and time invested in things like Chamber of Commerce meet-and-greets produce business in the long run. 2) The occasional client lull is a reminder to expend some of my

advertising budget; i.e., spend the time to get my face in front of people.

As with any investment, you need to look at what works for you and what does not.

> I have used Chamber of Commerce meetings as an example. Living in a metropolitan area, I have held membership in several local Chambers. After a while I migrated to other organizations and relationships. I have not been mercenary about it; I do not join or participate solely for access to potential clients; I do my best to provide value in each circumstance; but I am also aware that I need to use my time wisely.

Bottom line, if a strategy is not producing clients—you have given it a fair chance and it is not working—stop and do something else. Move your investment around, keeping in mind that it **is** an investment; and like any investment, the dividend varies based on the nature of the investment vehicle. Keep my original caution in mind, it is not a waste of time just because you are not making money in the moment.

Money hidden in a mattress is protected from market downturns and bad investment decisions, but neither can it grow or produce a benefit. So, take your time 'out of the mattress' and put it to work for you.

Actual accounting: Revenue vs Expenses

It is outside the scope of this book to go into detail about even simple financial accounting. A course at a local community college or online can help you learn the basics of bookkeeping. Most important as a business owner, you need to understand the elements of a profit/loss statement and how to read a balance sheet.

Knowing and understanding pertinent financial data will make or break your business. Too many of the people I counsel have never created a profit/loss statement, which is critical to running a business. Too many have no idea how much money they have in the bank or how much debt they hold.

You need to know the inflow and outflow of money in your business. If you lack a healthy relationship with money, you cannot go into business for yourself. If you don't know what you are looking for, it doesn't matter what you get. Such ambivalence toward the financial aspects of your practice leads to frustration. Unclear goals and lack of conviction in your ability to practice leads to a sense of poverty, you never feel like you have enough.

You live in fear, the fear of not knowing. Anyone acting out of fear automatically defaults to the negative, a sense of not having enough. If you do not have enough for yourself, you resist allocating any of your meager resources to service providers, convinced that you can save money doing it yourself.

In terms of doing things for yourself, there are certainly business functions you can take on yourself, but what is the cost if you make a mistake? And is there really a return on that investment? Someone who knows what they are doing will do it knowledgeably and efficiently, allowing you more time to do the things you do well.

Business School Primer

Businesses take many forms. Even in hypnotherapy, you will meet people with a variety of business models. Everyone begins with the same questions. What are your needs? What do you need to get out of the business? If you don't know, it's a good time to start figuring it out. If you don't care—maybe you are just in it to have a good time—relax and enjoy it; but acknowledge that that is the definition of a hobby.

With that said, even when you approach the business of hypnotherapy with sincere, earnest diligence, you can expect to make mistakes. Hopefully you can benefit from the adage, "The smart man learns from his mistakes. The wise man learns from the mistakes of others."

> Acknowledging that I strive to be wise, but am sometimes merely smart...I share the following 'Business School' experiences.

Know how much money you need to bring in, your fixed costs, how much money it takes to stay afloat.

> I had a business advisory client involved in a medical practice. I estimated the first $10,000 of patient fees each month went to paying basic expenses. That included the rent of a fancy office, paying several employees, equipment leases, etc., a big hole which amounted to servicing debt; and with debt comes interest.
>
> The business was losing money hand-over-fist. I suggested he shut it down. He refused. He didn't want to let down his employees. Yes, he was honorable, but all it accomplished was to delay the inevitable.

Don't forget to include a paycheck for yourself. What is the minimum wage you want to earn for engaging X number of hours per day, week or month in the business?

> For several years I sat on a business advisory panel called "The Boardroom;" half a dozen successful CEOs giving advice to entrepreneurs. The most common scenario was as follows. A struggling business owner would explain that he had rationalized basically donating his work until the

business was on solid footing. Now a few years later, the business is still emerging; he doesn't want to charge his customers more, he doesn't want to pay his employees less, and he has whittled away his own savings and the contributions of family and friends. He puts in an 80-hour workweek for peanuts. Then (here's the kicker), when we ask what advice he wants from us, he wants to know how he can expand his business (add more locations, start a franchise, etc.). His assumption is that growing the business that way will create wealth. Again, "His assumption…"

Everyone who faced us tried to convince us of their passion, and they did indeed have passion in spades. What they were missing was basic knowledge of business. Passion cannot make up for a lack of knowledge.

To make a business out of hypnotherapy, you need passion for and knowledge of hypnotherapy. You can get by on less passion for the business side, but you cannot get by without some business knowledge.

If you cannot meet the fixed costs, including paying yourself adequately, it is more practical to shut down the business, get a job and continue hypnotherapy as a hobby. At least you won't go in the hole financially. Why engage all that time, energy and effort just to have debt!? You can find ten other ways to have debt without having to work so hard.

As with my hair stylist, you need to figure out how many clients it takes to meet your fixed costs. When you get there, stop. She says, "I do not want to own a beauty shop. I don't want to own a building or be the boss. I am my own boss."

She rents a nice space, a work station in a spa, paying $400 a month regardless of whether or not she has business. That is her fixed cost. She doesn't have to pay for electricity or water. "I do two color jobs a month and that pays my rent. The rest is icing on the cake." She budgets for supplies; the lotions and potions she uses on clients; and she has to maintain a set of tools. She does not have healthcare insurance herself, but has it through her husband's work

She has established for herself the amount of money she needs to be happy. It takes four days a week to make that money and she loves her job.

She has created optimal conditions in terms of the space she rents. Clients are willing and happy to pay at the rate she charges. She maintains a steady stream without having to advertise.

She has control of her working environment. By charging a fair rate and taking off the time she needs to recharge, she is carefree when working with clients. It is highly sustainable. Clients return because they get a quality product for a fair fee. She is able to sustain her enthusiasm and creativity because she has the work/rest ratio where it needs to be for her. As one of her many happy clients I am delighted to give a larger than customary tip each time.

As in hypnotherapy, her work is creative and every client is different. It works for her, but it would not work for everybody.

This book presumes you want a six-figure income, but some of the preceding information may have you wondering if you might be better off doing hypnotherapy part-time. Maybe you have a spouse whose employment provides benefits. If so, they would not need to be included in your business costs. That changes the calculation and your business goals would probably be different.

Another scenario is that you are working in a way that you receive benefits and do not need your hypnotherapy business to cover them. That is not the same as owning a whole business on your own. The costs are not realistic. If your plan is to leave your current employment to go into hypnotherapy fulltime, you need to consider how those costs will be covered.

That was one of the harder nuts to crack when Steve left his last university position to join me in the business full time. When COBRA coverage runs out you discover how much you take healthcare-coverage-as-a-benefit for granted.

There is no one-size-fits-all. Most people graduating from a training program are told to charge $120 - $150 per session. Some people charge more, some less, depending on the market. But it is just an arbitrary number if you do not have a budget and have not set specific goals.

A Groupon for a local hypnotherapist offered 75% off his normal fee. What happens with Groupon is that you are required to sell your service at a minimum 50% discount and Groupon's share is half of that.

Let's say the hypnotherapist's normal fee is $100 a session. At 75% off Groupon collects $25 and gives him $12.50. If 100 people make a purchase, the hypnotherapist receives $1,250. The presumption is that he will give Groupon customers the same level of service as any other customer. If he follows the industry standard of a two-hour first session, he has to devote 200 hours of his time to earn that $1,250. That comes to...bring out my calculator...$6.25 an hour!

Yes, a few Groupon clients will convert to the $100 rate; but that is only after he has worked the equivalent of five forty-hour weeks at well less than minimum wage.

How is he going to deliver that service and be excited about it? After the first 10 sessions (half a week's work for $125) he will be demoralized and tired, and no longer doing a good job.

It's not always a good goal to have just a lot of people show up. Ask yourself how you want to be viewed.

> I purchased a Groupon for a massage. Knowing that I was to receive $100 in service though I had paid only $25, I felt bad for the masseuse. She was probably receiving less than $10 for that hour. It became quickly evident her heart wasn't in it. I left feeling like I had wasted $25 and an hour of my time.
>
> I have a personal policy of not discounting my fee. I do not use the word *discount* when talking about my work. The minute I do it devalues my work. It is disrespectful. I recommend you take the time to determine a fair fee and stick with it. You will be happy doing the work because you are not shortchanging either the client or yourself. No discounts. No freebies.
>
> If you choose to give a session as a gift, that's different; it is a choice, yours.
>
> I hate sending out reminder notices to get payment. The service is already gone. If you have to send a reminder for someone to pay you, for the most part you will not see a dime of it. People who are honorable would have paid up front. People who are honorable would not allow themselves to take your service and not pay for it.
>
> If you allow someone to take your services and pay later (which—unfortunately—they rarely do) you are facilitating theft. You are inviting someone to steal from you.

I do not trade and I do not discount. Okay, even though I say I don't, once in a while I slip. But when I do it comes back to bite me and I get a rude awakening, "Kweethai, take your own medicine." Do not discount. Do not trade. Do not bill. Get payment upfront and deliver your work with joy.

Chapter Review

This is a short book. A longer book might describe a bunch of ways for you to increase revenue. But that is not the problem for most hypnotherapists. The hypnotherapists who are struggling to make a living are generally sabotaging themselves. They undercharge. They are shy and self-effacing. They assume the role of caregiver and floor mat, afraid to speak up for themselves lest others may reject them. It all comes down to low expectations.

To earn 6 figures you must require a respectable fee. You must be confident and bold, yet kind and compassionate. You must assume the role of professional service provider; someone who lifts others out of the pit to a higher place, while keeping a respectable boundary. You direct your therapy sessions because you are the professional. You attend keenly to your business, because otherwise there is no business.

Chapter 8 - How to brand YOU

What makes you stand out?

Branding is about emphasizing the most unique aspects of your work. Branding is much easier for me to do with a Business Advisory client live because I am able to probe and examine. This forces the client to recognize aspects of themselves they would not otherwise consider. I want them to come away from the process saying to themselves, "Wow! I'm pretty darn good!"

Instead of attempting to describe that process in detail, the following are a couple personal examples. The first describes how I developed my own personal brand. The second describes how I applied reflection and analysis to solve a marketing problem.

The meaning of the *Dr. Kweethai* brand

When I left academia and went into hypnotherapy I adopted a new identity as *Dr. Kweethai*. Most people in academia knew me as *Dr. Neill*. The *Dr.* title in *Dr. Kweethai* maintains my professional identity. It gives the client an instant frame of reference, that I am well educated and well trained. I carry it with pride. It has substance behind it.

Clearly I worked very hard to earn the PhD, and it is appropriate and relevant to the work I do as a hypnotherapist since my PhD is in health promotion and adult education. Hypnotherapy makes up only a portion of the services I offer as a health consultant and change catalyst. Since my work is so closely related to my training as a health educator, the academic title is appropriate.

For someone with a doctorate in a field totally unrelated to hypnotherapy, whether or not they still use the academic title is up to them.

Then there is the phenomenon of people outside academia with nontraditional PhD's. That would be any PhD earned not through a conventional, traditional, tertiary institution. Such degrees are usually completed in a much shorter time and with minimal rigor.

> You might wonder if it really makes a difference where a PhD came from. To get licensure for my hypnotherapy school I had to complete an application with the Texas Workforce Commission (TWC). Two of the candidates I listed on my board of advisors were rejected by TWC because TWC did not recognize the source of the "PhDs" after their names.

Doctoral studies are not the right path for everyone. Yes, it has helped me; but if you do not have academic degrees you simply have to explore other options to convey your 'authority'. I know many highly successful hypnotherapy colleagues who do not even have college degrees but who are very good at what they do. They establish their authority by their competence.

As for *Kweethai*...Neill is a traditional, formal surname, but it is not mine. Whatever last name I carry has been some man's name; belonging to either my father or my husband. My original family name is Chin. I changed it when I came to this country and became a citizen. The judge at the ceremony asked if I wanted to change my name. My children carry the name of Neill (my spouse at the time), so I chose to change my last name to Neill as well. I carried that name and was published under it as a researcher and professor. Under those circumstances, I decided not to change my name anymore.

When I re-married, it was to Steve Stork. He is a man who did not need me to walk around with his name, and I had chosen not to change my name anymore. So when it came time for me to practice hypnotherapy I decided to use my first name. It is the only name I can call my own.

Now, some marketing people will claim it is difficult to spell and say. I do not need every person in the street to be saying my name. I only need it to be meaningful to the people who seek my services. I have not had a single client who could not pronounce my name.

The brand name *Dr. Kweethai* has become meaningful. It does take a bit of effort to learn to say it, but if I could learn to say Elizabeth, clearly you can learn to say Kweethai; it is only two syllables. When necessary, I easily teach people how to say it, "It's like *queen* without the *n* and the *tie* you wear around your neck." It is two simple syllables.

As a brand name *Dr. Kweethai* combines both a sense of familiarity and formality. *Dr.* is the formality. Using my first name is the familiarity. That is consistent with my practice style. It is important to maintain professional boundaries. I do not allow clients to address me by first name only. *Dr. Kweethai* allows for a certain boundary we do not want to cross. Clearly I am the expert. That is why they seek my help. I want to always maintain that degree of formality.

I have had clients who are also colleagues. I ask them in a public setting to address me as *Dr. Kweethai*. But in private settings they are allowed to call me by my first name only. When working in a therapy setting with them; where I am consultant, coach or change catalyst; reverting to *Dr. Kweethai* is appropriate.

Chief Catalyst for Change

I spent a lot of time, effort and money to come up with the word *Catalyst*. In a chemical equation (remember, I was first trained as a scientist) chemical reactions may occur fast or slow.

Applying a catalyst to the equation accelerates the reaction, saving time if the planned reaction is typically slow. However, while the catalyst accelerates the reaction, it is not otherwise involved in the reaction, and in the end remains unchanged itself. I see *catalyst* as a wonderful metaphor because that is exactly what I do. I do not get involved in a client's struggle. I stay outside the pit. And yet, with my being there, I help the client quickly achieve the change she desires. So I am the *Catalyst for Change*.

I like the idea of being the *Chief Catalyst* because I may have other people working for me someday. Or, since it is my gig, I am the Chief. Instead of calling myself the Chief Operating Officer, or the Chief Executive Officer, I am simply the *Chief Catalyst for Change*.

Hypnotherapy in branding

Hypnotherapist is on my website as a keyword search term, but hypnotherapy is not emphasized as my primary identity. I am more than a hypnotherapist. The process that evolved from my work, IChange Therapy, is inspired by the ancient book of changes, *I Ching*. That book teaches us about the natural changes in life. My work is about facilitating change. I help individuals grow in the direction they wish to grow. iChange is a pun for I Ching. Also, people who know about the *I Ching* instantly draw a reference.

> As a health educator, my work is to help individuals make healthy changes in their behavior and lifestyle, so they can live a life with the ability to cope with whatever challenges come up. Living a life without stress is not living. The only place in this world where there is no stress is six feet under the ground. As long as we are alive there will be challenges. The difference is to live a better, healthier life; knowing that whatever challenges come your way you have the

confidence to deal with them without hurting yourself or others. That is what I teach as a health educator.

The hypnosis portion of iCHANGE THERAPY helps the client get past fear energies that prevent them from being the best they can be. I use hypnosis to work with the client at the subconscious level, to resolve fears embedded in their mind that come back to haunt them, that come back to bite them, and that prevent them from doing the things they want to do. The hypnotherapy portion is to dig them out of the pit they have found themselves in.

After that; the part missing from much of hypnotherapy training; is what I call LIFE ENHANCEMENT TRAINING. I find it crucial to help the client navigate the world she finds herself in, so she does not go back to where she was when she came to me looking for help. Clearly, finding oneself in a state of suffering can be attributed to the accumulation of bad decisions. What got them there in the first place? What is directing decisions in a way that is not in their best interests?

At this point clients need to learn a new way to make decisions. If nothing has changed other than the fact that they have been fished out of the pit of despair and suffering, it is only a matter of time and geography before they get back to where they came in, only this time in a slightly different way.

In iCHANGE THERAPY the initial piece of work is to get the client out of their suffering. After that I go into teaching/coaching mode, LIFE ENHANCEMENT TRAINING. I teach the client new ways to communicate, how to speak up for herself, learning how to tell certain people to leave her alone when they are not serving her in a positive way. I teach her how to tell the negative people in her life, the porcupines, to piss off (but do it elegantly).

A whole set of assertive communication skills is crucial to being able to live with the revised energies the client has achieved after hypnotherapy. That includes how to make better choices in her own best interests. Most bad choices are due to fear. In fact I count almost every bad choice as resulting from fear. So, if I can teach a client not to be scared, she will make better choices for herself. She will have more peace of mind.

The final piece of iCHANGE THERAPY is environmental balance. In order to live in a state of harmony, the interaction between the client and her space is very important. Sometimes it means moving from the physical environment she is currently suffering in. Sometimes it means moving away from a relational environment. This is where I engage the ancient Chinese science of FENG SHUI. It helps the client redesign, recalibrate or reconfigure harmonious physical environments.

The components of iCHANGE THERAPY work together to help the client find peace and harmony within herself and also within her spatial environment. Getting healthy and happy inside out using this three-part process is a feature of my work that evolved over time. Somehow it came about as I began to practice hypnotherapy. It is as if I spent my whole life training for it. When I found hypnotherapy, and discovered what it could do, it felt right. It was the missing piece.

After 11 years of helping so many people through the use of this methodology, I know that it works. Former academic acquaintances tell me I should set up an evaluation process and write articles. I tell them that is no longer my job but theirs. I am too busy actually helping people. I don't need to prove that it works. It only matters to me that my clients know.

In conclusion, my practice employs a hierarchy of brands. IHEALTH CENTER FOR INTEGRATED WELLNESS is the name of the business. Each word was painstakingly selected and debated; including *for* vs. *of*. I introduce myself as *Dr. Kweethai. Chief Catalyst for Change* appears on my business cards and promotional materials as a supplement to my academic credentials. ICHANGE THERAPY is the particular approach I use when working with clients. LIFE ENHANCEMENT TRAINING reflects my professional knowledge and expertise in health education. FENG SHUI is not my brand, but it is consistent with my Chinese heritage and knowledge of energy medicine.

As someone looks at me as a possible service provider, strategic use of that branding terminology makes me stand out from possible competitors.

Two more things about branding

In your website and social media you have to use recognizable, generic terminology for people to find you. Imagine walking into Barnes & Noble; you want to find a book by a particular author; but books are not categorized by author, they are categorized by topic. You have to know the topic you are looking for.

Reverse that process when searching for a service provider. People searching for you do not know YOU exist. They are actually looking for someone who does what you DO. So, in terms of website and social media, you have to help people find you through what you do, applying terminology such people are likely to use.

The main keyword search term on my business website, www.ihealththerapies.com, is *hypnotherapy*. I do not like to refer to myself as a *life coach*, but it is part of my keyword profile because I know that is a term many people who would benefit from my services are likely to use to find me.

Branding then, is what makes you unique and stand out in that category. *Chief Catalyst for Change*, iCHANGE THERAPY, and LIFE ENHANCEMENT TRAINING are hooks that draw potential clients to read more on the site. A literary hook is a technique used to draw the reader's interest, to make them want to know more.

Creating a market leader: Pitted prunes in the Malaysian market

A long time ago I was a product manager for a very large marketing firm in Malaysia. I branded consumer products. I found out quickly that branding is all about making something about a product stand out. For example, one of my twenty-two product lines was pitted prunes imported from California. How exciting can you make a box of pitted prunes!?

It turned out to be my best product line. What I did with that line of prunes gave me the nickname Kamikaze Product Manager. According to my boss I had the gutsiness of a samurai. Coming from him, it was high praise as I was the first and only female product manager they ever had, which meant having to work five times harder than my male counterparts.

Malaysia is a multicultural country. Prunes are an imported product. The market leader at the time was made by a big-name company. It was top-of-the-line and had the largest market share. I initially shared the common assumption that a box of prunes is like every other box of prunes. A prune is nothing more than a dried plum. Regardless, I bought a sample of every box of prunes on the supermarket shelf. I took the prunes out of their boxes for a taste test and a visual examination.

The market leader had its top-of-the-line reputation, but no one conducting the tests could tell any difference in visual quality or taste between the actual prunes once you removed the boxes and brand names. However, I noticed that our prunes were slightly larger than the market leader. Plus, even though our product was priced significantly lower, the packaging was of better quality. The top half of our box was wrapped in gold foil. If you did not know the history of the two products, and simply compared boxes, our box *looked* more expensive, and that implied better quality.

When I asked my boss why our prunes were priced significantly lower than the market leader, he replied it had always been that way. The former product manager just felt that it was second to the market leader. There also had been a fiasco. A whole shipment of the imported prunes was lost to mold when the cooling unit in a refrigerated warehouse malfunctioned. People were unreasonably scared of the product.

Decisions based on fear are never good. So I ignored history and just analyzed the quality and packaging of the product in front of me. I was determined that we would become the market leader. My boss perked up, wondering how I would accomplish that. I explained, "In every aspect of the branding we are superior and unique; so I am going to double the price. I am going to make us the most expensive box of prunes in the market." The whole marketing team shriveled up and started looking at their shoes.

At the time I was blissfully unaware of the last product manager's experience with these prunes. Anyone who had gone through the experience with him considered me quite insane. They anticipated I would not last three months with the company. Who could blame them?

I asked my boss to trust me and allow a very large order. The new marketing campaign would establish our prunes as the new market leader. He said, "Woman, I stuck my neck out to hire you. I am sticking my neck out to support you now. If this flops, your head is on the chopping block and so is mine." I promised not to let him down.

I proceeded with the campaign. We leveraged the packaging, which was already superior to the current market leader. We raised the price to make it a premium product. Then we flooded the market with it during fasting season in the Muslim community. Muslims eat prunes to break their fast. As a food scientist, I knew they did this to stimulate the salivary glands.

Instead of attempting to market our prunes to every culture, we focused on Muslim customers and launched the campaign during the month of Ramadan. The packaging was gold and blue, as blue is a good color for the Muslim community. Establishing it as a premium product meant people would buy it as a gift to exchange with each other.

That campaign expanded my company's yearly sale of prunes from 48,000 to 2.5 million Ringgit (Malaysian currency). Therein I won the title of Kamikaze Product Manager.

Marketing strategy

The underlying strategy of such branding is that people want to buy quality and are willing to pay for it. The product already had the quality and appearance.

Applying this to your hypnotherapy business, branding yourself begins with self-assessment. What do you already have that is better than someone else out there? What can you do? You have to find at least one or two unique features. What is it about you that sets you apart in the marketplace?

In my box of prunes, the internal quality was superior, even if that meant it was just a little larger. Bigger is better. The packaging material was also superior. Gold foil packaging was more expensive; which didn't influence the quality of the prunes themselves; but made the product appropriate to exchange as a gift.

We already had something uniquely of higher quality than the market leader, so why were we priced significantly lower? Price reflects quality, so to make my prunes the market leader I focused on that perception. The new pricing set it apart. Launching it during Ramadan in festive packaging was a natural fit with customers' inclination to gift-giving; and, between the price and the packaging, it was a gift that could be shared with pride.

The product was previously mispriced due to limiting beliefs. The former product manager did not have the confidence to go after the market leader. In order to be successful you have to have good leadership. You have to have vision. You also have to understand consumer psychology.

You cannot lead others if you cannot lead yourself. Trust the vision you have for yourself and take a leap. First, overcome limiting beliefs and set prices appropriately. Second, do not just rely on price, but position it to be successful. Price, position, promotion; people based.

To be perfectly clear… Price your hypnotherapy services appropriately (no discounts). Then design and position your marketing of those services to meet specific needs, based on a specific client profile.

Proficiency and people

What value do you give clients? What are your special skills that give clients value?

> I spoke on the phone this morning with a potential client. It wasn't until the end of the call—we had already identified an appointment date—that she inquired about my fee. I

told her what it was. It didn't faze her. I told her she was worth it. She told me I was worth it.

The prior steps in the book are leading us to this. You have identified your skill. You have identified your audience. Now, in terms of branding and marketing, you are identifying your audience and how they are going to find you, using search terms relevant to their needs. Branding is simply how you appeal personally to the client that you want.

> Someone recently asked me who my competitors are. And I had to respond that I didn't know. Maybe I was just being polite, the real thing is that I do not mind competition. My process and personality are different enough that clients who would best benefit from my skills are drawn to me somehow. I might even say that the Universe sends them whenever I am ready for the next case.

So, identify something unique about you.

- How do you practice? NLP, Elman Technique, Transforming Therapy, etc.
- Where do you practice? Maybe you are the "only hypnotherapist on" the Front Range, or 57th street; location might be important to potential clients
- Why do you practice? Maybe you have personal experience with rape/incest, alcoholism, pain, etc. that makes you uniquely qualified
- Do you have a relevant credential? BS, MS, PhD, MD
- Have you developed a special expertise? iChange Therapy, Parts Therapy, Regression Therapy, Sports hypnosis...

If you can't figure it out for yourself, ask friends and former clients. Something has to be extra special about you and how you do what you do...

I choose to operate on the promise of being the premium market. Look at Lamborghini, do they have competitors? Few if any. Someone seeking a Lamborghini will just walk up and purchase it without price shopping or comparing features with a Ferrari. It is a unique marketing process that is uncommon. Do you dare to be uncommon?

> My fee strategy is uncommon and not without risks. But 1) I have done the math and 2) I deliver on the promise implicit in that fee. The way I work, it is not possible for me to see lots and lots of clients and still do a good job. I work one case at a time and set a price where I don't have to work every day of the month. It allows me to live the harmonious lifestyle I choose. I love my work and my clients love the results they get. And, I also have time to enjoy my garden and my family.

The challenge is to appeal to people who will benefit from your services and can pay. The right clients are happy to pay. Anyone who calls and asks for service based on price alone (huffing at a fair fee) is not the right client. You have to be willing to let that person go.

> Depending on your point of view, that may seem harsh or greedy. 1) Harsh: I am turning away someone who has asked for help. 2) Greedy: They do not have enough money to be worthy of my time.

> Neither is true. Rather, I am recommending that you make it a goal to stay focused. If you want a 6 figure practice, you have to keep your eye on the ball.

> Most often it is not price that clients balk at. Rather, they need to be educated to value the work. Clients get very creative in coming up with the means to pay when they can see the value you provide. That also means they value

themselves enough to engage. The best clients are people who gladly pay for your services because they value what you offer them.

Transmute harsh and greedy to magnanimous and professional. 1) Magnanimous: Make a referral to another hypnotherapist who can provide adequate service at a price point matching the client's budget. 2) Professional: Reserve your time and energy for clients who expect to pay a premium for high value service.

If you still feel guilty about maintaining a respectable fee, make it part of your schedule and financial plan to accept a certain number of cases on a volunteer or *pro bono* basis. The point is, you choose who and when.

> I had to learn that the hard way. There have been times, out of either fear or compassion, I have allowed a client to walk in without being able to pay the full fee. It has never worked as well as when a client has to stretch to come up with the fee; because the client who goes to that effort feels she deserves the process. The fee I charge, no matter what walk of life a client is in, is a respectable chunk of money. There are other ways to spend it. But when the client makes that choice; that she is worth it; therein is the first level of success, to engage.

Go for the right client

> In the prune example, I wanted to be the market leader; I didn't need to take over the entire prune market. I only wanted a specific chunk of it – the premium sector. People not interested in the premium product at a premium price still had other options.

If you do not have extraordinary skills, you cannot charge a premium fee. If you do, it is called fraud. On the other hand, if you have the skills, do not feel guilty about asking for what you are worth, ask the appropriate fee. When you know your client values you, and you don't have to worry about who will pay your utility bills and rent, you can focus on giving your best work to the client.

Make it personal

Decide on three things you do exceptionally well. Then imagine the type of people you can help. WHO are the people who would be willing to engage your services, value them, and happily pay for them? That is the foundation of your personal brand. Decide on those unique features, then align all your marketing efforts at sending a consistent message. After you have identified your client and developed the brand, you have to position opportunities for the client and brand to interact. Set the intention and send the energies out to those who will receive them. Avail yourself to meeting your clients.

Chapter review

Work through limiting beliefs to determine what your skills are. Engage pricing appropriate to those skills. The combination of skills and pricing directs clients to you who will best benefit from your work. Once you have determined your skills, pricing and clients, you need to start thinking about keywords; how will you attract clients?

As you start developing your brand, think of it as a compass that guides clients to you. No matter where you are, the compass points to you. You are true north for the right clients.

You have to develop the perception that you are uniquely qualified to help the right clients transform and change in the ways they desire. The brand-as-compass (as well as any sub-branding) should all be done with an eye toward clients you want to attract.

Effective placement is critical when potential clients are looking for the service you provide. When faced with multiple choices in the marketplace, you want clients to be attracted to **your** brand.

A third possibility of an effective brand is that it commands the attention of people who are not looking specifically for your service, but your brand and presentation promote the idea that they may want to learn more about it. It compels them to find out more.

The result of all this is your marketing plan. Your website and all promotional materials much include your branding, keywords and skills. When that marketing plan is all integrated and appealing, you are ready to launch.

Lessons from a Roll of Toilet Paper
If you behave like a roll of toilet paper, don't complain when you get used for its intended purpose!

I had settled into a new office in Georgia. We bought a house on Tomlinson Road, in a town called Milledgeville, having relocated my practice in Hypnotherapy. What a mouthful! Imagine the number of times I had to spell out my new address, but also 'hypnotherapy', to people who had never heard of it.

We moved from the Dallas-Fort Worth Metroplex, from a large university campus, to a rural town in Georgia, to a tiny college campus. My husband had taken a faculty position more aligned with his teaching interests. So; lock, stock and barrel; we moved. After a year of successful practice in north Texas, I was faced with starting all over.

I found space in a long row of professional offices, much like my set-up in Denton. This time I did not buy the property, not yet knowing the town or the people. I thought I would rent for a year and let Steve settle in before I made any significant real estate plans. As luck would have it, my office was about the same distance from our home as the Denton location had been.

I signed up with the local Chamber of Commerce as an easy first step to gaining access to the local business community. The Chamber Director twice asked me how to spell Hypnotherapy. How in the world was I going to build a practice in a town where folks couldn't even spell hypnotherapy!

It turns out Milledgeville was a very pleasant university town. The business community was open-minded and kind to me. I met the president of the local bank and we quickly became friends. Still, I was new in town, I looked different, and I offered an unusual service. I attended Chamber meetings and began giving lectures around town. I was eager to get working.

I met Tina at a Chamber meeting. She was into some kind of multi-level marketing. One morning she volunteered to give me a ride to a Chamber meeting. It turned out her office was only a few doors from mine. After a couple more outings and morning coffee, I discovered Tina's business was not doing well. She was losing money and in debt. Her husband was on disability and they had eight children at home.

I felt bad for her and offered to help. She told me she did not have the money then to pay for my services. I was so eager to help her I told her she could pay me over time. We could arrange a payment plan so she would pay me something every month. We agreed on the payment plan and I gave her a few sessions. She benefited from the sessions and thanked me. I was happy about that.

When payment day arrived, she showed up and dutifully paid me twenty dollars. I did not mind; I was just happy she was making payments. Yet that changed. After a couple months she stopped paying. I reminded her nicely on several occasions, and she just as nicely responded with one convenient excuse or another. I negotiated, telling her I wouldn't mind receiving two dollars a month; but she must keep her word. At the end of that third month she looked me in the eye and said she simply could not pay anything further, she just did not have any money. I decided to let it go. I felt rather bad she had used my services without hesitation and then left me feeling like a nasty bill collector.

A week or so later a friend invited me to a clothing party. Julie's business was to organize a tea party at a hostess's house, do a fashion demonstration, and then sell women's clothes. I had a schedule conflict and did not attend. A few days later, at least two weeks after Tina told me she could not pay me, I called Julie to ask how she did at the sales party. Julie was thrilled. She had met Tina at my office and invited her to the party. "Your friend, Tina, came and she was my best customer. She purchased more than $350 of clothes; and she paid cash! Thank you for introducing her to me."

I was stumped! I was speechless. She what? I swallowed my surprise, finished the call with Julie, then sat silently for minutes. It took me awhile to fully gather my feelings. I felt betrayed. I felt used. And I felt humiliated.

I felt dirty. For the first time I could imagine what it feels like to be a piece of used toilet paper. People wipe their dirty bottoms on you and discard you with no hesitation. Betrayal. Betrayal!

Of course I was angry at Tina. I felt she had done wrong. I was furious.

I decided to call a good friend who lived in Chicago. Dana had studied Feng Shui with me years ago. I maintain great respect for her person and her spirituality. Dana listened as I ranted about my "Tina issue." The more I ranted, the worse I felt.

As my fire expired, Dana responded very calmly, "As your friend, I am going to suggest something. You may not like what you are about to hear but I want you to know that I am saying this to you because I am your friend and I love you and want you to grow."

"Uh-oh," I wondered, "what's Dana going to do to me, now?" I couldn't see her taking my side because, somehow, deep in my gut, I knew all this ranting and raving was not exactly good energy! "Okay, Dana, let me have it. What did I do wrong?"

"It's is not about what you did wrong, it is about what you did not do right."

"Wow, that is an interesting perspective. First, Tina used my services and then she lied to me. And now you tell me it is something I failed to do? I am floored."

I could hear the love in Dana's calm voice, "Kweethai, what part of this responsibility do you bear?"

"What do you mean, what part of this responsibility do I bear?"

"What did you do to attract a client like Tina into your life?" I was stymied, so she continued, "Don't answer me right now. Go home and think about it. You will find the answer. Call me in a couple days if you don't, but you will KNOW it when the right answer comes to you." And thus ended my conversation with Dana.

I was greeted at home by my eternally cheerful husband. He is always happy to see me at the end of the day. Yet, on this day, I gave him a quick hug and put him off for thirty minutes, "I am going to the bathtub to consider something very crucial. Not to worry, I will be fine...see you in 30 minutes no matter what."

Off I went to draw a hot bath, dumping in half a bag of Epsom salts. Usually two cups suffice, but I needed a stronger dose to pull out the bad energies; and there were heaps of bad energies in me. I settled into the hot water, taking a while to adapt to the heat and finally allowing the soothing warmth to work its way into my body. I calmed myself, closed my eyes and settled into a serene trance.

So what about me attracted Tina into my practice? I was new in town and was living in fear that if I did not choose my clients I would have no clients. I did not do my usual screening with Tina. Hypnotherapy is not for everyone and certainly not for folks who have no intention to pay. I needed a client more than Tina needed me. It was the wrong formula!

It was my fault to offer her sessions on credit. It was my fault for offering services without taking payment upfront. It was my fault to tell her it was okay to make even smaller payments.

Tina treated me like a piece of toilet paper because that is how I presented myself. She wanted to clean up some doo-doo and I handed her the roll. What right did I have to be surprised!

OK, I get it now. It took about twenty minutes soaking for me to get it, and another ten to forgive myself. I had to fess up my mess before I could clean it up. As I *got dressed, I told Steve we would eat out to celebrate after I finished one small task.*

I returned to the office, took out Tina's file and brought it home to my back garden. I said a blessing, lit a match to the file, and released both Tina and her debt to the Universe. I took responsibility for the issue and decided that I would not chase after Tina any more. I paid for it as a lesson in business. As the file burned to a small pile of ash, I felt a sense of relief; the burden of fear was lifted from me. I knew from then on I would trust the Universe to send me clients whom I could help and who would be happy to pay for my services.

Chapter 9 - What resources do you need?
Set yourself up for success

Many business startups fail due to lack of planning for the resources to facilitate the first phase. I call the first three months the seeding phase. It may be longer for some businesses. You have to engage a lot of time, money and effort to get the business launched. During that time you need a cash reserve to cover operating expenses, assuming you do not immediately generate revenue. If you bring in money, great; but you must plan contingencies.

Total how much money you are going to need for the basic expenses of just opening your door. The basic costs of opening your door include rent, utilities, phone and website. Some services require a deposit. Make sure you have that, then double it to be conservative. Then add an additional 15 to 50% as a margin. That may seem like a lot, but financial resources give you peace of mind, particularly when you do not have clients yet.

This is particularly prudent if the practice is something you plan to make a living from. So, in addition to covering all business expenses, you need to account for your personal living expenses as well. You have to be able to pay yourself.

What is the minimum amount of money you need to sustain basic living expenses? That is the minimum you need to pay yourself. Let's say you need $3,000 to pay your bills and carry on your current standard of living. That is the amount you must bring in above and beyond your basic business expenses. You may be able to cut some costs, but do not incur too drastic a change or you risk getting yourself into a pit of fear and poverty.

Once you have a basic budget and funds to carry you through the seeding phase, put all your energy into building business and attracting clients. That starts with providing value and quality service that helps clients achieve the results they want. It would be nice if you could step back and just enjoy being in practice. But, since the practice is also a business; you cannot just lock the door as you follow the last client out at the end of the day. Being in business means you must constantly be on the lookout for resources that allow you to stay in business.

Resources come in many forms

For the first three to six months of your practice keep in mind you are establishing the level of operational quality and service you will provide ongoing. You want to convey that in your marketing and promotion. You want to enhance it via professional memberships and conferences.

> The last thing you should trim is attending professional conferences. Most people think it is unnecessary expense to attend conferences. I consider conference attendance crucial to your practice. It puts you in touch with your community of peers. It puts you in a place where you can learn new skills, meet new people and rejuvenate and refresh your energies. Going to conferences should inspire you, not scare you. It is a place to be nurtured, so go.

You may also need money to consult a coach. A mentor can point you in the right direction and provide occasional advice (more details follow below). In contrast, you pay a coach to teach you the right skills and keep you moving in the right direction.

Bare minimum, you need a dedicated space

Imagine you are the client. What kind of surrounding do you want to be in? The office must look professional. The client must feel safe and comfortable in your space, with the ambience of a safe, trustworthy and professional space. It must look, smell and feel clean. It has to have the appearance of a place you would want to be.

For some people that may be very clinical, something like a medical office. Other people's offices look like something out of a temple. Others look like a mystical cave, or maybe an upscale hotel lounge. The way you present your space depends on your earlier planning, how you want to be perceived by your clients. But any physical settings needs to help your clients feel safe and comfortable.

In an economically depressed area, having a very posh office will push people away. In a very upscale area, having broken furniture will be a turnoff for paying clients. It is all part of your image and branding. Everything contributes to that image.

You need a computer and printer to print out bills that look like professional bills. You need a website. These days a website is as important as having a good business card. It is a virtual business card. To not have a website today is similar to if you did not have a phone forty years ago. Clients contact you through the website, or get your contact information. To not have a website immediately creates a question in the potential client's mind in terms of professionalism and credibility.

If you have a limited number of dollars for marketing, invest it in building a quality website. It is the most efficient marketing tool you will ever have. The website content, appearance and ease of navigation must all be consistent with the way you want clients to perceive you. Some people have very fancy websites, but an office that is very plain. That is an inconsistency that creates doubt or fear, lack of confidence in you as the practitioner, and there goes your client.

Furniture

Practicality of furniture is critical. If you are going to work with weight loss, you better have a chair large and strong enough that a weight loss client does not break it and hurt himself. Then consider suitability, color and style.

Make your furniture an extension of who you are. You don't need to take out a second mortgage on your house to buy expensive furniture, but the furniture has to be clean, functional and respectable if that's the image you want to put out.

> A friend invited me to visit her hypnotherapy office. She had vinyl-covered furniture; with broken legs, duct tape covering the torn bits, stains, etc. Newspaper and magazines were strewn about. Alternative healthcare products were arranged haphazardly. It was a cross between an employee break room and a Goodwill store, not a professional office. The bathroom was no better. She charged below a three-figure hourly rate, but that is still no excuse for not addressing basic hygiene.

> I once interviewed an accountant as a potential service provider for my business. I could not find a place to sit down in his office. Every surface was covered; it looked like he was hoarding documents. He was friendly enough and seemed knowledgeable, but it occurred to me, if he could not keep his office in order, how would he keep my accounts in order? It made me uncomfortable and I did not hire him. Sure, he had clients, possibly lots of them, but he didn't get my business.

Other less than obvious resources

Build a network of people who can help and support you in your efforts. That is why professional organizations are important, for you to meet people and engage a circle of peers who can help each other with questions and problems. It is good to have a mentoring relationship with a senior practitioner. If you don't already, you may want to hire and pay for, in a contractual relationship, a senior practitioner to be your professional coach.

In getting from where you are to the next level of business, it is important that you seek counsel from someone more knowledgeable than you. Peers can only help you to their own level of practice. So when you need serious advice, you need to be willing to pay for it. Make sure it is from someone who has been there, done that, and been successful. But also be mindful that it is disrespectful to expect free advice from someone who makes their living dispensing such knowledge.

Always be careful from whom you seek counsel. Consider; when you want to lose weight, all your friends become nutrition experts. It is hard to help someone lose weight when you are overweight yourself. A smoker cannot help a smoker quit smoking. That goes back to the beginning. Know thyself.

> A recent acquaintance was promoting a new service to help middle-aged singles navigate the dating scene. In conversation he revealed his own inability to sustain a long-term dating relationship. He spouted statistics and quoted self-help books, but it was quite evident he had been unable to apply those strategies in his own life. Most surprising was that he was not aware of the contradiction; that he was trying to build a business with himself as an expert on a topic at which he was currently a failure. An idea is great, but delivery of the idea requires one to have proven expertise and competency in order to convince others of the idea's value and validity.

There is value in having a peer coach when you select someone who is already where you want to be. You don't want to select someone just like yourself. You want a hero. You want to model after someone you admire and respect, someone with more skills, knowledge and wisdom than you. You want someone who is DOING it.

> Einstein opined that a problem cannot be solved at the same level at which it was conceived. If you desire to get to a higher level of practice or business, find a guide who has *been there*.

What advice, specifically, do you need?

As you are getting started you want a second set of knowledgeable eyes to look at your documents and forms; your space, furniture and clothing; doing so from the perspective of a client. There are things you cannot see for yourself; personal preferences that may not be shared by clients; that only the peer coach can see.

> That doesn't mean you need to follow everything they say. There have been times I disagreed with the advice of a counselor I was paying. I went ahead with my choices, but it helped to air out differences in opinion.

It takes a good mentor or coach to not impose and insist that you do exactly as they do. Rather you want someone who will help you air out and compare ideas, allowing you the freedom to make the final choice. You have to make your own choices, because no one else can take responsibility for those choices.

Just because you are learning from someone who has experienced success does not mean you have to do everything exactly as they did it. You are an individual, with your own strengths. A poor teacher puts you in a box that limits you to their limits. A great teacher helps you expand the box, encouraging you go to your own level of competency.

For me, having had a crazy idea, I could look at my mentor, sitting back and smiling, as encouragement. He had confidence in me that I was not able to see in myself. That is a sign of a good mentor. He believed in me when sometimes I did not believe in me.

A good mentor also points you in the direction of more knowledgeable resources. Your resource list has to be about more than just money and time. Consider the arena of influence. When you experience a very specific problem, you may not know who has the knowledge or expertise to help, but your mentor likely does. That makes it crucial to be connected with the right people.

Professional Membership & Conferences

Membership in a professional organization should be a requirement for anyone claiming to be a professional. It is just as important to attend that organization's conferences.

Conference attendance is somewhat an art of its own. Beyond the obvious function of providing a venue for continuing education and training, there are governance meetings and social gatherings. Briefly, to get the most out of a conference; do not just attend sessions, submit proposals to share your own expertise with others; attend committee meetings to participate in the governance of the organization; use the social gatherings as an opportunity to meet new people and, more importantly, to allow people to get to know you.

> It is not a holiday. As an academic I took students to conferences. I took one advanced graduate student in particular, hoping to present her with networking opportunities. Though I had reminded her the conference was to be considered work, not a vacation, she took it as a personal holiday and chose to sleep in rather than attend a

As a teacher, I look forward to when a student's level of competency eventually exceeds mine. I want to delight in facilitating that success. I can be proud to say I helped facilitate growth of the creative endeavor. But their success is their own, not the teacher's. My job has been to help clients emerge into their best self. As a Catalyst, I emerge from that process unchanged.

If you start to recognize limiting beliefs in a mentor or peer coach, it is time to look for someone else. There may be things you want to do and the mentor says it won't work. In some cases, of course, they are right. But you have to analyze the reasons underlying their resistance. Is it their own fears, or their fears for you? Are they imposing their own limiting beliefs on you?

In any given lifetime you need just a few mentors. A mentor is a lifelong relationship. Mentors should be judicious in their advice.

When I was in graduate school, my mentor Dr. Dinero would sit back in his chair, put down his sandwich, ponder a moment and smile at me, "That seems like a very interesting idea. I wouldn't know how to make it happen, but if anyone knows how to make it happen, I believe I am looking at her." In that moment I could see he recognized and respected that I had talents he did not have.

Just because he could not see the solution did not mean there was not a solution; but since I came up with the idea he gave me the responsibility to find the solution. His advice was to not not do it, but to pursue it and see what happens. It was then up to me to either fly with it or flop. Either way it was my responsibility, glory or failure, my choice.

very important breakfast meeting. I was amazed (and not just a little disappointed).

The work at a conference is to create opportunities to meet people who can serve as a resource in the future. These are people you may call due to a particular expertise. As the need arises, your call begins with a reminder that you have met and had a conversation. It is not a cold call. Rather, it is someone you have had at least a brief encounter with (and hopefully made a positive impression). These types of encounters at a professional conference establish your professional bona fides.

In my early days, as a member of the American School Health Association, I met an influential woman at the annual conference who worked with the USDA in Washington DC. She took a liking to me. She was much older, knew everyone, and insisted on dragging me to a bunch of meetings. She insisted I become a committee member on her Council. She later facilitated me becoming president of that Council.

She also took interest in my progress as a new professor. She gave me very good advice along the way without telling me exactly what to do. One remark in particular helped me turn down a position with the federal government; though it would have paid twice as much as I was currently making, it did not suit me well. I am ever so grateful for connections like that, that saved me from wrong choices.

I have had many little angels watch out for me. When I need to compare or confirm something I already know in my gut, messengers from the universe give me good counsel. Of course, you have to be open to receive it, and then you have to take action.

Chapter Review

What is the most important resource to your business success? You. If you are not the success you would like to be, it is a reflection on You. It may be a self-fulfilling prophecy ("I lack confidence.") or you may still be growing you knowledge, skills and competency. Acknowledge your current state and make a plan. There are innumerable stories of people who started in meager circumstances yet went on to become wildly successful. As you get to know a mentor they will describe their own difficulties getting started. They will often speak fondly of their own mentors. Only a few people sprint to a 6 figure practice. For the rest of us it is more like a marathon. By all means, look forward to the finish line, but don't forget to enjoy the run.

Afterword

The intention of this book has been to share with you my path in hypnotherapy, how I built a successful practice, and some suggestions if you want to follow my example. If you have a passion for the work, and plan to be very successful, that is a good start. But business acumen and marketing skills are essential to make it work out. Then there is a secret ingredient to this recipe I have alluded to but not discussed directly. It is something outside the typical hypnotherapy or business tool box. Once you discover and master the secret ingredient, it may not matter whether or not you achieve a 6 figure practice, because you will decide you are already successful.

Money is just a number! This idea has been with me all my life. Perhaps it came from my father or mother or some wonderful teacher I do not remember. As I embraced the concept, I threw fear out the window.

My mother gave me the gift of trusting in my own being. "Nothing can define you but you." "Ask and you will receive." "Be still and know that I AM." These, and many other adages, populate my consciousness and come in handy whenever I encounter a crisis.

So, while you aspire to a 6 figure practice in hypnotherapy, do not be limited by it. I wish for you boundless blessings and a consciousness of abundance. There is plenty out there. But you must ASK. Then you must be ready to RECEIVE. Because God delivers quickly if you are open to it.

Let me end with this book with a lesson from the Universe.

God Delivers faster than FedEx

I decided I never wanted to relive being used like toilet paper. I determined to only accept clients who paid ahead. That way I didn't have to feel bad when a client was late or didn't show up for an appointment. Since they had already paid, I could go out to a nice lunch on their time when they decided not to show.

One Wednesday I set aside time to do my bookkeeping. I discovered a few old receivables for which invoices had been sent in hopes of collecting. I had implemented my new payment policy, but these were old client accounts. "Yuk... I am sick of sending out bills to people who simply ignore them. It is degrading and disrespectful to me."

I know some people communicate directly with God, but it wasn't part of me. Yet, I found myself unconsciously talking to God. Actually, it was not unconscious anymore. I became aware I was indeed addressing God. No one else was with me. I had locked the office door so I could do my paperwork undisturbed. It felt good, so I continued.

"God, I hate having to collect from people who are dishonorable. Can you; can YOU; yes, I mean YOU; GOD, please; PRETTY PLEASE; send me only clients who value my work, who can benefit from my work, who respect and honor me, and who PAY me in cash!?"

In those days I did not use credit card merchant services, so clients paid by cash or check. Once in a while a check bounced. So I added, "Oh, and can you please have them pay for services in advance? It is hard to foreclose on services rendered."

I thought about it for a moment while gazing at the crystal hanging above my desk, "Yes, God, that would be really nice." Before I could fathom another idea, there was a knock on the door. It was December and cold outside. I opened the door and, staring at the person before me, my mouth flew open like a cod fish. "Hi," he said with a wide grin, "hello, I am Samuel and I am here!" It was a face of pure delight. Samuel was short and ruddy-faced with a white beard and sparse bits of white hair on his head. He was either Santa in disguise (absent the red suit) or Santa's head elf. "Dr. Neill, I am here!" he declared again.

The man knew me! But I did not know him or how to reply. "So you are here!" I repeated back to him. "Please, come in, it is cold outside." The chubby little fellow followed me inside and I offered him a chair. "What can I do for you?"

"My wife Sandy and I attended your lecture at the Herb Garden Center two Sundays ago and we were very impressed with your work. I am here to sign us both up so you can help us lose some weight."

I recognized it was now time to implement my new policy and told him I required prepayment for my services. He did not hesitate. Jumping out of the chair, he pulled out his wallet and placed a small pile of greenbacks on my desk. "I will bring the rest when we come back. See ya!" And he turned to leave.

"Hey, wait a minute. I need to give you a receipt and book your appointments. I need some information from you such as name and address." He scurried back, completed the paperwork, and left again; as I stared in wonder at the pile of cash.

Looking up again at the crystal, I screamed "Oh my GOD!" In that instant I almost heard "Yes?" "Thank you God, you delivered faster than Fed Ex!"

With that, I bid you success! All you have to do is ASK!

Best Intentions,
Kweethai Neill, PhD
April 27, 2015

About the Author

Dr. Kweethai Neill's academic and professional careers span over 40 years. She has dazzled audiences, inspired students, helped clients heal, and facilitated business achievement, at home and abroad. Dr. Kweethai is Chief Catalyst for Change and founder of iHealth Center for Integrated Wellness. *iChange Therapy*, her methodology for personal transformation, integrates hypnotherapy, communication training and Feng Shui to help clients get healthier and happier inside and out. She is author of, *Hypnotherapy, An Alternative Path to Health and Happiness.*

Over the decades Dr. Kweethai has published numerous articles in peer reviewed and professional journals, and has created many training programs and DVDs for health promotion and leadership development.

Dr. Kweethai holds a PhD in Health Education from Kent State University, an MS in Nutrition from Kent State University, and Bachelor of Science with Honors in Food and Management Science from King's College, London University. She was Associate Professor and Department Chair of Health Studies at Texas Woman's University; Faculty of Health Promotion at the University of North Texas, and tenured Professor of Health at Sam Houston State University.

Dr. Kweethai is happily married to Dr. Steve Stork, who is also her partner in business. She enjoys cooking for friends, growing beautiful flowers and herbs, reading, traveling and playing with Steve and their granddaughter.

They live in Roanoke, Texas.

Dr. Kweethai's Trainings

Please check our website for latest events.

www.ihealththerapies.com

www.drkweethai.com

Contact us if you wish a customized training for you and or your group. Call 817 491 9809

301 Main St, Roanoke, TX 76262

LIST OF DR. KWEETHAI's Offerings

Hypnotherapy: An Alternative Path to Health and Happiness

- ☐ Hard Cover Book — $29.98
- ☐ Audio Book (MP3) — $29.98
- ☐ BUNDLE: HARD COVER & AUDIO (save $10) — $49.98

LESSONS IN LOVE – DVDs

- ☐ How to Talk so your Partner Will Listen — $29.98
- ☐ How to Find and Keep True Love — $29.98
- ☐ The Big O — $29.98
- ☐ BUNDLE: all 3 titles (save $15) — $75

ENERGY MEDICINE MEETS HYPNOTHERAPY TRAINING SET

- ☐ Mayaguez, Puerto Rico - 2 Day Training — $299
- ☐ Las Vegas, Nevada - 1 Day Training — $299
- ☐ Working with Client with MS (4.5 hours) — $299